The Unfiltered Guide to Working in Wine

The Unfiltered Guide to Working in Wine

Hillary Zio

To order additional copies of this book, contact:
Xlibris
1-888-795-4274
www.Xlibris.com
Orders@Xlibris.com
748834

Contents

To my parents, for never giving a damn what career I chose and supporting me always.

Chapter 1

Introduction

I'm guessing you're reading this because you want to break into the wine industry but don't know exactly where to start. You like wine, you want to know more about it, and now you're thinking of making a career out of it. Maybe you've worked in one sector of the industry and now you're curious about another. After reading this, hopefully you'll know how and where to begin, the work you can expect, and the necessary steps and requirements that will land you in your ideal position.

I've found that the new generation of wine enthusiasts are itching to get into the business and there wasn't a real and current career guide out there. As an Educator, I feel that it is my duty to share my knowledge and experiences. I'm not a Master Sommelier, and I don't have a PHD but I'm a Certified Sommelier and I know my stuff. More importantly, I have worked the majority of wine jobs out there. After a decade of training and working in wine, I can honestly say that there is a serious need for enthusiastic people. Furthermore, there are plenty of options for anyone interested, and that's why I decided to write this book.

This guide was inspired by my peers, colleagues and acquaintances that weren't new to the workforce in general. They've worked in finance, advertising, or some other industry and were dying to get out and do what they love. These people have been mostly women, which is interesting and also great to see in this male-dominant industry. Guys, it's great that you're reading this and you'll get just as much out of it, I've just personally recognized the need for this information by women.

Many of the aforementioned women have expressed their fears about leaving their corporate job to explore something in wine. While there *are* corporate wine jobs, I wouldn't go out looking for them, at least not in the beginning. Truth is, stability and the wine business don't always go hand-in-hand. For example, I've never received healthcare working in wine. This has more to do with the size of the companies in which I've worked than anything else. Small restaurants, retail stores and distributors rarely have the means. A lot of these women have also taken a fat pay cut to get into wine. For these reasons, I might recommend saving up before your first attempt into the industry. Throughout this guide, you will see why a baby bundle of cash will help you start out, within any sector.

Also, I don't delve too deep into what these jobs pay. This depends on so much, but especially physical location. Also, if you are interested in working in wine, you shouldn't be too concerned with big paychecks (at least for a while), sorry. You should be here because you LOVE wine, find most of it insanely interesting, and want a career doing something you love each and every day. The way I see it, if you have to be somewhere most of your life, why work in a job you hate? People seem to have this notion that working in wine is luxurious, and it absolutely can be, but it's more of a way of life. You'll taste some great wine and food, travel to some beautiful regions and meet wonderful people, but you probably won't buy yourself a Ferrari.

I've separated this guide into sectors of the wine industry (Restaurant, Retail, Wholesale, etc), but I highly recommend that you read all chapters, as there are similarities on the selling and the buying side within each category, several tricks of the trade and interviews that can be applied throughout. Speaking of interviews, four of my most passionate and successful friends agreed to be interviewed throughout this guide.

Not only is the wine business enormous, I've also found that it can be whatever you make it. You might be looking for a job as an auctioneer or a vineyard photographer or anything else super amazing, but I'm focusing on the big picture today. This book is based on the majority and most common wine careers, so that you can understand where to begin. I recommend getting creative as hell, with the end goal of doing exactly what you love the most.

Chapter 2

My Background

I actually started in Porn...

Got your attention? Good. Let's back up and start this story on my last day of college. From since I can remember, I was always very into fashion. I had the shopping addiction, read every fashion mag on the stand, followed the trends religiously, and figured it was the only place to look for a career for myself. I didn't want to, like, make anything though. Upon graduating and with my new Economics degree, I figured I'd go into buying and analytics, I mean it's just shopping right? Wrong. So here I am, 21 years old on my last day of school and looking for fashion jobs... in Tempe, Arizona.

Here I go: www.Craigslist.org (enter) Buyer Jobs (search), "Assistant Buyer Wanted: Duties include: Assistance in the purchasing of: clothing, accessories, shoes, swimwear, and other related products for our 13 locations nationwide. Company: Undisclosed." PERFECT, (apply)!

With my short resume consisting of just a few local clothing stores, a high school accomplishment and a sorority, I was surprised to be contacted the following day. He asked to meet at the local Starbucks to discuss the position further. Over coffee, the head buyer let me know that the company was within the "adult" industry. Okayyy... So I was to be purchasing clothes, shoes and accessories... FOR STRIPPERS. On top of that, the "other related products" included sex toys, condoms and pornographic DVDs. He mentioned that my work would be done at their headquarters, and that I need to be efficient in excel. He also mentioned that I would need to go to Vegas a few times per quarter.

VEGAS? Oh this 21 year old is SO IN! So I went on and on about how I'm "totally cool with that" and I "know all about that stuff," resulting in some pretty odd facial expressions. We laughed a little and boom! I was hired on the spot. For over a year, I replenished the sex toy cases, reordered the Jenna Jameson DVDs, and saw a ton of really weird shit. It didn't take more than a few Vegas trips to realize that this probably wasn't for me. Finally, my then-boyfriend-now-husband and I decided to move to New York City.

While desperately looking for work in fashion, I started to become fascinated with wine. I think this was due to the massive selection and options throughout the city. I will always believe that being half-way between the old world and the new world, Manhattan is the best place to learn about wine. As an adventurous eater, I couldn't believe all of my dining and drinking options. Let's say you want to drink Hungarian wine and sing karaoke at the same time. Well lucky you, there's a place for it on the Upper West Side.

Without any sort of wine-related experience, not a serving job, nothing, I began to look for work. Where better to start than the city's only winery. I applied and was accepted for a seasonal internship, assisting the winemaker and his team. The grapes were shipped in from California, and the 6 of us would sort them, press them and punch them down. The majority of this internship, however, involved cleaning barrels and washing tanks. I loved the lab work and checking the juice for various reasons (mainly alcohol, to ensure that the fermentation process was going as planned). I was exhausted at the end of each day, but I learned way more than I ever imagined. There's something so fascinating about witnessing the transition from grape mush to wine.

The other interns at City Winery were studying at the International Wine Center. This school in mid-town follows the WSET program, which I'll discuss further in the next chapter. I followed their advice, that it was the only real wine "school" in the city and signed up for the program. I had also been told that to become a Sommelier, you need to get your certification from the CMS, which I will also discuss. So, I decided to do both at the same time due to the content cross-over. I would compare this process to a two year Associates Degree, having been 22 with no experience.

At the end of the internship, and destined to find my place in the wine world, I started looking for a job as a Sommelier. Now, this internship was literally the only experience I had, so I knew that I'd need to work as a server before the title and role of a Sommelier was a possibility. This is true almost 100% of the time, keeping in mind that all restaurants are completely different.

Finally, I found the perfect opportunity, a new wine bar was opening, by none other than the first female Master Sommelier, Laura Maniec. I had actually taken her course in preparation for my first, Introductory CMS exam. You'll come to find just how small this industry is. After several interviews, I was hired as a server at the new, Corkbuzz Wine Studio (a restaurant with weekly wine classes). This came as a shock since I had such little experience, but I had just passed the Certified Sommelier exam weeks before (Level 2) and my enthusiasm was no joke. For over a year as a server and learning from Laura and the rest of the seasoned staff, I was asked to join the "Wine Team." Ecstatic, I was now responsible for organizing the cellar, monthly inventory, fetching bottles, and even some ordering and replenishing.

One evening, when Laura was too ill to teach a class and the other Sommeliers were unavailable, she called me to fill in. I was thrilled but insanely nervous. Thankfully, the class, Food and Wine Pairing went very well. Afterward, I just wanted to teach as much as humanly possible. I loved helping people find their palate and teaching them about everything that makes wine so interesting to me. They shared my passion, we'd have long and fulfilling conversations, and speaking to a group about wine was totally invigorating. Weeks went by and I wasn't able to teach many classes. I didn't take this personal, as Laura is a Master and had two Advanced Sommeliers (Level 3) there to teach when she could not. So, I went to find a place where I could focus all of my energy on wine classes alone, and that's when I found New York Vintners.

Not a restaurant, New York Vintners is actually a wine shop with nightly wine classes and they were in search of a full-time teacher. After being hired as a part-time teacher, I was quickly promoted to full-time, and then as the Director of Education. I absolutely loved coming to work Wednesday to Sunday, noon to 10pm. For over two years, my Friday and Saturday nights involved educating large groups of people on wine. I had such a great time doing it that I didn't even notice how little time I spent with my friends and even my fiancé. He went off to work each morning, I was coming home past 11pm, and our days off were never the same. After two years, I finally realized that it was taking a toll on our relationship, and I was out to find a day job with weekends off.

At this time and with over four years of experience in the industry, I started making some solid connections. These were people that I'd met at tastings and reps that came to me weekly with new ideas for the list or shelf. One female sales rep in particular became a good friend of mine and still is to this day. Over several of our wine bar dates, she would spill on her happiness on the seven years she'd spent as a rep. It became quite appealing to me. She creates her own schedule and always has nights and weekends off. After several conversations, I decided to follow her advice and went looking for a career in distribution.

You'll read more about these three, main sectors of the industry and where I am today in chapters to come. For now, let's make sure you know your stuff.

Chapter 3

Where to Get Certified

So you saw the SOMM movies and you still want to study wine? Welcome back to school. It's a big-ass world of wine and easy to drive yourself insane. It's never-ending, and you can literally dedicate a lifetime to just one country or even one wine region. Get ready to delve back into history, geography, geology, science, and so much more...

First, a college degree usually helps. Even if you party your way through college and decide on the easiest degree, most companies like to see that four year dedication. Does the wine industry really care what you study? Maybe, but probably not. Some are certainly more impressive than others, but if you are looking for a job in sales, buying, or managing, you can't go wrong studying some type of Business. I have also found that several wine careers require extensive writing and some more-than-basic computer skills.

Wait, do I even *need* a wine accreditation?

Some might tell you that experience is everything in the wine business, but I think that a structured wine education helps immensely. In this competitive day, it could be the deciding factor on whether or not your resume gets pulled from the pile. I know plenty of successful people in the industry that could be Master Sommeliers if they wanted to, but they just don't care. It's very expensive and probably just a stupid little pin to them. Many of these successful people are a bit older with a lot of experience. I often find that newbies to the industry who don't choose to go through some type of education run into a lot of hurdles. For example, they work in a French restaurant for 3 years and decide to work in a retail shop and know absolutely nothing about Italian wine. At least with an entry level certificate they understand major regions, as well as the particular grape varietals and climates within. That said, sure you can skip it, but you better work.

Around 40 countries produce wine today, and you should know 15 of them inside and out. Studying the wine producing regions within each country is nothing like studying their political regions. Consider what you studied about France in High School. Well, there was Paris, the Alps, and The Atlantic Ocean on the left side. Maybe you described the country in North, South, East and West terms, but that was about it. Now, you'll see France separated into wine regions: The Loire, Rhone Valley, Bordeaux,

Burgundy, Champagne and all of the sub-regions inside each. You might even forget where Paris is, seriously. So where should you study and/or get certified, and how does this apply to what you eventually want to do in the industry?

A.) "The Court"

Within the Court of Master Sommeliers, there are 4 levels, each one is light years harder than the next. After passing the fourth, you can call yourself a Master Sommelier. Keep in mind that only about 200 people have passed this exam, which goes up by just a few each year. This is inarguably the most well-known wine certification program. Since it is so recognizable, I would sign up for the Introductory Exam (level 1), if you have not passed it already. Keep in mind that they tend to book up three to six months in advance. Same goes for the Certified, if you have passed the Intro, as you must pass each exam in order to move on to the next. The breakdown looks like this:

1. Introductory Exam (level 1)
2. Certified Sommelier (level 2)
3. Advanced Sommelier (level 3)
4. Master Sommelier (level 4)

The Introductory exam is for the candidate with a general understanding of wine. Not that they could pass on that alone, as this level requires a two day course before the exam can be taken and the test questions stem from the course. The first day, you listen to a few Masters speak on wine (broken down by region) from 8am until 5pm. You taste around 25 wines during these lectures, as well as speak to the group (of over 100 people) on the wine's sight, nose, palate and conclusion. You don't want conclusion, unless of course you know damn well what the wine is. The next day, you repeat the process until 5pm when you take the exam. This 50-100 question test is multiple choice and based on the materials taught over the past two days. Example of a test question: Mendoza is a winemaking region in what country? A.) USA B.) Australia C.) New Zealand D.) Argentina. Yes, the answer is D, good job.

Level 2 is the Certified Exam and there is no two day seminar, or even one day. This is much more intense and difficult to pass. Unlike the first level, you are tested on tasting and service, along with the exam (multiple choice, fill in the blank, matching, and more). You must pass the Introductory Exam to apply, and you need to know about every major winemaking region and grape varietals. Not only wine, you'll be tested on beer, spirits, fortified wine, common cocktails, cigar service, and more. Here's how this test goes down:

You are given 1 white wine and 1 red wine and told to fill out the "tasting grid" completely in a matter of 15-30 minutes. The sooner you're done, the sooner you can start the written exam. As soon as you complete that, you will be given a time to come back in for the service portion. Service is nerve-racking to say the least. You walk into a room, and it's just you and a Master Sommelier. He or she pretends that there are other people at the table (imaginary friends... very strange) and you are told to open wine, possibly decant, and serve the "people" in order of the Court's service standards (guest of honor first, then women, then men, and finally, the person who ordered). During this time, you are asked several questions about wine, cocktails, beer, pairing and anything remotely relevant. If you don't know the answer, you can reply, "Let me check with the bartender on that one," but I wouldn't use that option more than once or twice. As mentioned, this can be a little terrifying. In fact, let me tell you about my experience.

I was a hopeful Sommelier from New York City and just flew all the way to Boulder, Colorado for the exam. Nervous as hell, I slept MAYBE 1 hour the night before, although I had been rigorously studying for over a year. My anxiety was on full blast, as I'd heard nothing but horror stories from friends and co-workers going into it. "You know it's a 30% pass rate, right?" "Oh, you've never bartended? Good luck!" "I hear they make you saber a bottle of Champagne in front of all 100 candidates." That last one is completely untrue, and ridiculously unsafe for that matter.

Anyway, the tasting was first and I thought I nailed it. However, you never find out what the correct wines were. This holds true for other wine programs, like the WSET and for good reason. If you said Sauvignon Blanc, and my friend said Riesling, but turns out the actual grape was Pinot Gris, she passed and you didn't. How is that possible?? Maybe the region you decided on was too far from the actual wine, maybe your acidity call was way off... list goes on. Giving away the tested wines is a post-exam nightmare for any wine school, so you just need to trust that they know how to grade and aren't out to screw you over. After a mere 10 minutes completing the wine tasting portion, I was given the exam. Shit. There were 100 questions and I knew about 80. 20 of the questions had been pulled from my wine brain, but how? Crossings, types of rot, the origin of Albarossa... I swear I used to know this! An hour in and one of the last to turn in my exam, I was feeling less than confident. Since I was one of the last to finish, my third and final portion, "Service" was to be much later in the afternoon.

I walked around the hotel nervous as hell, studying exactly how to properly decant, open Champagne, fold a serviette, all of it. Finally, my name was called. I walked in, set down my backpack and locked eyes with my Master. He sensed my nervousness and tried lightening the mood by asking about where I worked, my flight, everything. As we got started and I opened the Champagne, poured it for his imaginary friends and answered any questions he had about pairing, cocktails, sherry, port and beer, I was feeling pretty good.

"Lastly, Hillary can you please fill 10 flutes with the rest of the Champagne in your bottle, pouring equal amounts of wine into each, and then walk around the table 4 times with the tray?" "Absolutely," I said, and set up my tray, poured into my flutes and did my monkey dance. As I walked back to him after my fourth turn, I tripped over my own backpack and the flutes came crashing down, one by one, for all of the candidates in the other room to hear. I stared at him blankly, then either nodded or curtsied, I can't recall. "That's all, Hillary. Thank you for your time." Welp, that was it. Everybody knows that if you drop, much less BREAK a glass of wine, you auto-fail. I picked up my backpack and didn't even ask what time the results would be announced. I was sure that I had failed.

On my way back to the hotel, I picked up a bottle of wine before bursting into tears. I called my boyfriend, told him I failed, called my best friend, told her I failed. The Certified exam was only held a few times per year, so not only did I need to wait, but I had to get another flight and hotel all over again. Two glasses deep, I looked at the clock and figured that the results were about to be announced back at the scene of the crime. I told myself to wipe my tears and go back, if just to say thank you and congratulate the others. I also needed to figure out when the next exam was being held on the East Coast because heaven knew I wasn't travelling this far for another let-down.

I walked into the room seconds before the three Masters began their lecture. "We want you to know that this is a very difficult exam for a reason, and that the certificate was never taken lightly. Only the best can wear the pin..." Then, 7th down the list, my name was called. Was I dreaming? Was I drunk? They actually said my name aloud. *I passed*. Confused, I slowly walked up to accept my pin and certificate and literally said "but I spilt everything and broke all the glasses." The Master looked at me smiling and said, "So what? It was pretty clear you know your shit." Take that as a lesson to obviously try your best in the service portion, but passing these exams will always be more about what you know.

Level 3: Okay kids, this is where I stepped out after 2 straight years of being waitlisted for the exam AND the course. That's right, there are two parts again like the Intro, but take place about a month apart. Maybe I'll keep trying, maybe not. I've realized that with my experience and the fact that I'm always studying for work anyway, that I may not *need* it by now. I just haven't been stumped explaining wine to my most serious and knowledgeable collectors. Most people go on from here because of personal goals, honestly. To even apply, you must have at least three Master Sommeliers write you letters of recommendation, as well as complete an application in regard to your experience in the industry. Every year, around 40 people pass this exam, held between one and three times across the United States.

Level 4: The Master Sommelier

After 7-10 years of study and only a 10% pass rate, only one hundred-ish people have passed this exam. That number goes up (by just a few) once every year after the exam is held (somewhere in the world). This test is by invitation only, and most candidates fail 7 times before the pass the whole thing. It's insanely difficult.

Like the Advanced (but without the course), there is a tasting, service, and written (sometimes oral) exam. The kinds of questions you can expect are flabbergasting and a bit ridiculous to some. But, they have to set the bar somewhere, because plenty of (crazy) motivated people all over the world are trying to be Master Sommeliers right now.

HOW MUCH IS THE COURT? (General estimate)

1. **Intro $525**
2. **Certified $400**
3. **Advanced Course and Exam $2,000**
4. **Master Sommelier Diploma (tasting, theory and Service) $4000**

The best way to study for these exams is by subscribing to guildsomm.com. You can probably find the answer to every question for the introductory, certified and advanced courses. They also supply you with maps, videos, sample tests, and more. The annual fee is $100 and it goes toward a good cause: wine education.

Another site I found helpful is Flashcards.com. You simply search their flashcard database by typing in what you are looking to study for: "Certified Sommelier" or "WSET Advanced" and you'll see tons of flash cards and sample questions.

Finally, get a mentor! In life, in business, but especially in your studies. Talk to people about what you should expect. When I was studying for the advanced exam, I asked my friend who is now a Master Sommelier, if I should honestly study *every* sub-region in the Rheinhessen (a region within Germany), and if each would be on the exam. He let me know that if there is something of note about the sub-region, then it is a test question contender. Why would anyone ask you to make long lists? It's about knowing what it is you are memorizing anyway. Perhaps there's a sub-region that specializes in red wine, which would be something to note, as it differentiates from the others that mainly produce whites.

Another example of wondering what to study: soil types. There are so many different kinds of top-soils and sub-soils out there, it's impossible for anyone to know all of them. However, common sense comes into play big time. When you begin to find out where you can find certain soils, you start to put them in similar climate regions. Napa, California and Bordeaux, France have many of the same soil types. This is due to the climate and latitude line, explaining why both specialize in Cabernet Sauvignon.

B.) "The WSET"

The Wine and Spirit Education Trust is quite different than the Court, but as you can probably figure, a large portion of what you need to know about wine carries over. The biggest difference between the WSET and the Court is that the WSET doesn't have a Service component. Well that's great for those who aren't interested in being a restaurant Sommelier, right? I would say that most wine students that decide to go the WSET route are interested in everything but service. They're looking for jobs in distribution, retail, marketing, PR and more.

The WSET Breakdown looks like this:

Level 1: Award in Wines and Spirits (Foundation Course)

Level 2: Award in Wines and Spirits (Intermediate Course)

Level 3: Award in Wines and Spirits (Advanced Course)

Level 4: Diploma in Wines and Spirits

Another important difference to note is that these aren't just exams with a one or two day course (like the Court is). The WSET conducts full-blown weekly classes (either in person or online) and the length of each class goes up based on level. They have a similar policy in that you are required to pass Level 2 before Level 3 and Level 3 before Level 4. You CAN jump right into level 2, however. Also, the WSET requires patience when concerning your exam results. I waited almost 4 months after taking the Level 3 Exam to find out that I passed. It was a long 4 months and I wanted to sign up for the Diploma but couldn't without my proof of pass. If you ask me, they should really change that. Students are way more likely to sign up for another class when the info is fresh in their mind and going to class becomes a habit.

Level 1: Award in Wines and Spirits (Foundation Course)

This is for consumers and newbies only, with a focus on pairing wine with food. There are 5 hours of class time total (in person only) before the very introductory, 45 minute multiple choice exam. I actually don't think it's possible to fail this exam.

Level 2: Award in Wines and Spirits (Intermediate Course)

A step up from Level 1, I would equate the difficulty of this course and exam with Court's Introductory Exam. There are 16 hours of class time and a 1 hour, multiple choice exam. In this class, you will learn about the major wine regions of the world, as well as the principles for tasting wine. The class is once per week for 6 weeks, but they do offer an "intensive" 2 day course and exam once per quarter as well. I would highly recommend taking that if you have worked with wine (in a restaurant or wine shop) for at least 6 months.

Level 3: Award in Wines and Spirits (Advanced Course)

This is much more intensive, and I equate the difficulty to the Court's Certified Sommelier Level. This is for those with a broad understanding of wine already; label laws, appellation systems, all of the most common wine producing regions and grape varietals. This involves 38 hours of class time (in person or online) and a 2.5 hour exam (blind tasting, multiple choice and short answer). The book for this class is great, but it is *heavy* on the technicalities of winemaking. So, whether you care about farming and science or not, you will be tested profoundly on each.

Level 4: Diploma in Wines and Spirits

After passing level 3, the Diploma takes between two to three years (on average) to complete. During these years, you may find that it consumes the majority of your weekends, if not your life. I'll be honest, I started the Diploma and ended up dropping out. Where I was with my career and family, I just wasn't ready for this kind of commitment. To break it down, there are six units: Wine Production, Global Business of Wine, Light Wines of the World, Spirits of the World, Sparkling Wines of the World, and Fortified Wines of the World. Also, there is an immense amount of writing and long essays involved with each Unit.

As I stepped away after the Advanced, my friend Jill Davis has agreed to answer a few questions about her experience in attaining the WSET Diploma.

---

1. **Jill, was the diploma process (courses, study time and exams) exactly how you imagined it? If not, what were some surprises or struggles?**

"I knew the Diploma was a rigorous program but I don't think I understood how many hours I would have to dedicate to studying. College was a breeze compared to this! For Unit 3, which is the most intense exam of the program, I was studying a little every day for about 5 months leading up. For the 2 months before the exam, I would ramp up to several hours a day, with all day sessions on the weekends. And for the couple weekends leading up, I was studying nonstop for 18 hours a day. The amount of material for this unit alone (and there are 6 total) is insane. The hard part is they can basically ask any question about any wine region in the world. Which means you have to study absolutely everything, just in case. And on the written portions of the exam, you are only asked a couple of questions, but need to provide as much detail as possible. Some of it is luck, if you happened to study a certain subject more, but a lot of it is just putting in the hard work to memorize as much as possible."

2. **What can you tell me about the WSET system that I wouldn't find online? Anything (good or bad) that you found about their approach that wasn't expected.**

"Something I've found interesting about the WSET program is how, at times, their preferences/opinions about certain wine regions show up in the syllabus. For example, the Jura region in France has hardly been mentioned in any class or syllabus in the 4 years I have taken WSET classes. Even though they've been making wine for hundreds of years. Another thing to note is that up until Fall 2015, when the new Oxford Companion to Wine was released, the Diploma course textbook was almost 10 years dated. Laws, regions, winemaking techniques, etc change all the time in the wine world. Because of this, there was constant cross-referencing of materials while studying. I would have the Oxford Companion open, while checking guildsomm.com and the wine region's website all at the same time to make sure I had the most updated information."

3. What would you tell someone who just passed their level 3 (Advanced) and wants to begin their Diploma journey?

"Start studying now! But really, study every opportunity you can get. It's a very large amount of material to memorize and the earlier you start, the better. Many people try to finish the program in a year or two and take several classes at once. I personally would recommend taking your time to learn the course work for each unit and take one at a time. Especially when it comes to Unit 3, that consists of 6 months of weekly classes and a 6-hour test. It's intense! And you don't want to have to constantly switch your mind from memorizing how to make rum (in the Spirits Unit) to memorizing Pradikat levels for German wine (Unit 3).

Also, make friends in your classes to study with. Tasting groups are key to your studies. You'll be able to taste a wider range of wines/ spirits as well as have other people to learn from. Another bit of advice would be to take every class seriously and try your best at passing the first time. You can take these tests numerous times but it costs money, time and lots of unnecessary stress. I know a lot of people who barely studied for certain exams and very much regretted it when they were in the exam and had to leave half way through because they didn't know enough to answer the questions. Some of the units are only offered once or twice a year which will also extend the time it will take you to finish the program. And finally, remind yourself that you're studying wine, and if you don't find it fun and fascinating, it's probably not the course of study for you."

The Master of Wine

While not associated with the WSET, the diploma is the pre-requisite. The Master of Wine exams are taken with the Institute of Masters of Wine. If you have received your Diploma in Wines and Spirits, you can be considered a Master of Wine Candidate. This designation is arguably equivalent to the Master Sommelier title. There are several written exams and tastings within three stages and takes most people at least 3 years. The pass rate is very low and there are only around 350 Masters of Wine in the World.

WSET Graduates and Their Options

The WSET program is wonderful, especially for those interested in working in the retail and wholesale sectors of the industry, as service is not tested like it is with the Court. Since passing my Advanced, I have found it recognizable throughout all sectors and even throughout the world.

I actually know a handful of people who have taken the WSET courses all the way through to the diploma but they have never worked in wine. Most of them want to eventually. They can tell you how to make wine and all about the rarest varieties in the world but some of them don't know their 'aias from their La Las, or even what DRC stands for.

You can study wine until you're purple in the face but without real experience, you might not be the best candidate as a Consultant, Buyer, or Sommelier. However, if you are interested in working for one winery, perhaps as a brand ambassador or winemaker, you might be able to slide right in with your WSET diploma. As long as the knowledge of several other producers is unimportant, you'll be just fine.

As far as retail and restaurant careers, knowing about producers is half the battle. On the flip side, do you think that every restaurant Sommelier knows about vineyard rot or brix requirement levels? Not unless they really went out of their way to study it. As someone who clearly didn't know what they wanted to do in the wine industry, I recommend a combination of both experience and education.

I decided to attain my certification with the Court as well as my Advanced Certificate (level 3) with the WSET. I also figured I'd double up and do them both, at the same time. I'd heard that these exams were very similar and everything was going to be fresh in my brain so I decided, why not? I even had several of the same questions on both exams, taken in the same month. They were equally as difficult, and I equate the time I spent on both to an intensive, two year Associate's Degree. Again, I knew nothing about wine before this point and peers with some wine experience have a slightly different comparison. It's also important to note that we all have different learning styles and test-taking capabilities.

HOW MUCH IS THE WSET? (General estimate)

Level 1: $370 (book, exam, etc)

Level 2: $850 (book, exam, etc)

Level 3: $1,700 (book, exam, etc)

Diploma: at least $7,000 (books, courses and exams)

C.) Other Certifications and Schools

1. **ASA (American Sommelier Association):** This is a fantastic option to become a Certified Sommelier. They offer mandatory course sections and tell you exactly what you need to know in order to pass. The only potential negative is that it used to be an easier and shorter process than it is now, so some companies do not know the current level of difficulty and dedication. I have heard that the exam is a bit

easier than the Court, and that they kind of give you the answers in the classes. Some recognize it as equal to the Court, while others do not. Many companies just haven't heard of it. There are 6 course sections, each takes around 3 months to complete (every Tuesday or Wednesday). Each course ranges from $1,000 to $1,500 per section. To complete all sections and exam, you are looking at about a year and a half to two years. I think this is a fine option, and have heard that if you can afford it, you will learn a ton and feel completely prepared to take your exam.

More info: *www.americansommelier.com*

2. **Society of Wine Educators** (to obtain a Certified Specialist of Wine (CSW) or Certified Wine Educator (CWE) accreditations)

    a.) **The CSW** (Certified Specialist of Wine) is a 100 question exam only. They offer testing locations at Pearson, located in almost every major city. I have heard that this is very difficult for someone who has not taken any WSET or ASA classes. You basically get a book and a study guide when you sign up for the exam and then study on your own. I would only recommend this to those who have not only taken classes, but also come with some experience. My good friend took this exam and said that it was slightly easier than the Court's Certified Exam, as there's no service portion.

b.) **The CWE** (Certified Wine Educator) is a wonderful option for those looking to teach, but this is a difficult exam as well. In addition to the Theory exam, you are required to do an educational presentation and successfully blind taste two wines. You can only apply for the program after you pass the CSW. Also, you must be able to finish each section within 3 years of signing up. This is also a self-study program. An interesting section of this exam is their "Faults and Imbalances" portion. They alter wines with chemicals and ask candidates to identify the faults. I think this is great, but takes serious experience, unless you buy the super pricey fault kit and smell each regularly –yum!

More info about both: ***www.societyofwineeducators.org***

3. **The ISG (International Sommelier Guild):** Wine Fundamentals 1 is for the total novice. There is one class and an easy, open book test. Wine Fundamentals 2 is taken next and takes 8 weeks before the essay-only exam. After passing Wine Fundamentals 1 and 2, you are able to apply for the Sommelier Diploma Program and call yourself a Sommelier Diploma Holder. This is a 6 month process, involving multiple essays. I'd compare the level of difficulty to the WSET Advanced Certificate, with more writing. There are a few interesting topic additions such as Menu Design and Investment Strategy. The downside of this program is that it is not very well known compared to the Court or the WSET.

If you like writing, complete this and then go take your Court Exams for recognition, as this will likely prepare you in full.

More info: ***www.internationalsommelier.com***

Some of My Favorite Wine Books

1. <u>World Atlas of Wine</u> (the new, concise version is best) by Hugh Johnson and Jancis Robinson. This is not for total beginners, as you might feel like you are reading in another language. However, it is essential for anyone studying regions and sub-regions.

2. <u>The Essential Guide to Wine</u> by Madeline Puckette is great for anyone beginning their wine journey. This book is quite approachable in describing a wine's structure, and identifying the differences in grape varietals.

3. <u>The Ultimate Wine Companion</u>, by Kevin Zraly is an excellent option for new students, as his uncomplicated language is refreshing. If you live in or near NYC, take his legendary 8 week class for $1200. He's been teaching it for over 40 years (!) and I've heard nothing but phenomenal things from everyone who has taken it.

4. <u>Wine Grapes</u>, by Jancis Robinson is a great reference for anyone studying varietals. I have also found her writing quite captivating and to-the-point.

5. <u>Exploring the World of Wines and Spirits</u>, by the WSET is a great book for any intermediate-level student. There's also a workbook connected to this book that can be purchased separately and great for testing yourself.

6. <u>The Oxford Companion,</u> by Jancis Robinson again! With worldwide acclaim, this is one of the best reference books out there.

   Books by Region: Once advancing and studying wine by region (which I recommend), there are several books you can buy on individual countries or regions. Truthfully, they can be a bit more difficult to get all gung-ho about unless a particular place seriously excites you. Some of my favorites are; <u>Vino Italiano, Makers of American Wine</u>, and <u>The Great Domaines of Burgundy.</u>

   Some fun ones: <u>Secrets of the Sommeliers, Billionaire's Vinegar, Wine and War, 1001 Wines to Taste Before you Die.</u>

It won't come as a surprise to know that the best companies to work for tend to take candidates with a background in higher wine education more seriously. This applies to most industries, but it's becoming more of a requirement in the wine business. Fifteen years ago, candidates who attended wine schools and held certificates were more of a perk. Even ten years ago, experience always came first. I believe that this changed when the newer and lesser known wine regions started making great wine. In the 1980s for instance, Chilean wine started to became very popular. There was a theme amongst the producers making good money, they were making good wine. All over the country, winemakers started lowering yields and getting rid of chemicals. This happened in the 90s in Australia as well, a turn for the better and we all appreciate it. This triggered a quest for knowledge by wine professionals everywhere. Now, you can be sure to find Chile and Australia in your course curriculum, resulting in well-rounded and open-minded wine students.

It isn't difficult to understand the importance of a well-rounded education, but here's a real life example: A friend of mine lived in Argentina for 10 years after graduating college. During his time there, he made wine for 3 different wineries and worked for an Argentinian supplier as well. He decided to move to New York City to continue his passion. However, he found he had an immensely difficult time finding work. His resume, while impressive, only consisted of Argentinian Wine. He figured, why should I get certified? I already know how to freakin' make wine! He had such a hard time getting work that he ended up pursuing the WSET Diploma and now teaches classes on every major wine region. His new passion for education stems from everything he learned, which of course he thought he knew originally. You'll soon find that it's imperative to learn about all countries that make wine, not just the one you live in.

Chapter 4

Wine Resumes and Interviews

Now, you're ready to start somewhere. I recommend Winejobs.com, Guildsomm.com, or good ol' fashioned Craigslist. There aren't too many other wine job websites or great head-hunters that I know of. Also, even if you just got a wonderful job in wine, always keep your resume current! You never know who you'll meet or what opportunities may come along. Also, if you haven't heard, people tend to move around very frequently in this industry. But before you start applying, take my resume building advice into consideration.

Your Wine Resume

1. List your wine studies first and foremost, including the course(s) you are taking with estimated finish dates. Then, list your college(s) or other education, then your experience. You might be the only

candidate dedicating time and money to expanding your wine brain. Let 'em see that first.

2. List everything! Since there is a lot of hopping around in wine, restaurant Somms and servers may work in a few different places per year. With wine shops and suppliers, it is slightly less common. The point here is that you shouldn't be afraid to list ALL wine related experience. We are the last to judge for holding too many positions within a short time-span. Sometimes, more is better and makes the interviewer think that you are well rounded and now ready for the position in which you are applying. You never know which wine-related experience you left out that could have been a conversation starter. After all, it's a relatively small industry.

No Experience?

1. Consider interning! You will see and learn so much, plus it can really beef up a newcomer's resume. Wineries are always looking for help. No wineries in your town? Ask a local wine bar or shop if they need an intern for the summer or the holiday season. You can intern at a restaurant one or two nights per week, helping print menus, check coats, etc. Since it will likely be evenings, you can intern while you work and/or study wine.

2. Look for gigs! Craigslist, Guildsomm.com and Winejobs.com usually have random, monthly or even seasonal gigs that could do wonders for your resume. Wine shops tend to hire "elves" during the holiday season. They pay by the hour to giftwrap bottles, pour at weekly tastings, and help pack-up holiday gift orders.

3. Hostess! Here's a great way to put a busy wine bar on your resume while learning from Sommeliers. Just look for the more educationally serious, wine-oriented spots. Also, I would look at the restaurant's wine list before applying. Do they carry enough wine from several parts of the world? It's important that you're learning enough and interested for at least 6 months of pre-shift meetings. If not, look elsewhere, as you should ideally want to be promoted to a server, then Sommelier.

4. You will have more of an idea of where to intern and apply for gigs or a career that best suits you after reading this guide, but don't be afraid to try several things. If I hadn't moved around so much, I'd still be wondering about everything I didn't try.

Interviewing

Don't be surprised to walk into an interview and be verbally tested on wine. As a manager looking through resumes, I'd always call the candidates with an ample amount of education and experience. But guess what?

People lie! So, wine quizzing is literally the only way to gage their level of knowledge. I often heard "I've actually just started studying," or "I used to study wine, it's been a while." So I would proceed to ask about styles of wine, varietals and regions. Things that any WSET Level 2 or Introductory Course (The Court) would know. Examples include: What is the grape in Barolo? Name two wine regions in the Northern Rhone. What is Sancerre? This is basic wine knowledge and very common on an interview. If they answer correctly, I'll ask harder ones. It can be nerve-racking, but there's really no other way to understand an applicant's wine knowledge.

People want to hire people they that they want to hang out with. Don't you like hanging out with people that are chill (aka not annoying or desperate)? They also have to know that you care. Be normal-eager as opposed to desperate-eager.

1. Over-dress, but look appropriate to the venue.

2. Know what to ask for. Don't go in with some crazy high salary requirement and zero experience to match. No matter where you have worked before, if you are brand new to the *wine* industry, you shouldn't be surprised to start at 40k. This was especially difficult for my friends starting in wine with backgrounds in finance. Don't be discouraged though, they are all doing phenomenal now, especially with that finance experience. Remember, you *can* make a good living in wine, it just takes time.

3. If the position requires "basic wine knowledge," that means different things to different people, but here's what it means to me: you know the top 20 most popular winemaking regions of the world. You know the top 25 most common varietals and blends in the world. You know what they taste like, why and how they taste different when grown in different places. Remember, you will probably be tested.

4. Be honest! If you are just starting to study, say so. At least you are taking this time and know the importance of it. Studying takes discipline and we in the industry respect that.

5. Ask away! When you don't ask questions in an interview, it's just as questionable as someone telling you that you got the job without having to interview. Remember to have standards. Ask them about struggles right now, how the team interacts, and what some of the company's goals are for the future. Interview them and they'll want to impress you. They'll probably get home that night asking themselves, "Why was I trying to impress them so hard? Oh, because I really want them on my team."

6. Comments can be awkward, make them into a question instead. Example: "I heard that you just received an award for your 2012 Cabernet." "Yep.... Sure did." Instead: "I heard that you just received an award for your 2012 Cabernet. Do you feel that this

was due to the vintage or all-around hard work by the team?" Here's a chance for a long answer that will undoubtedly help both of you.

7. Adapt to the situation. While remaining true to yourself, gauge the vibe and act the way the interviewer is acting. Being able to vibe on others is huge for sales positions and owners know that. Making the interviewer comfortable with you means that you will do the same for potential clients.

8. Send a thank you note! I was once told that I got a job because I had a messenger hand-deliver a thank you card to the office the day after my interview. I'd like to think it was more than that, but there is something to be said of going above and beyond. I recommend writing a thank you email after each interview that goes beyond "thank you for taking the time to meet with me today." How about after that sentence, mention some of the subjects addressed with additional points on why you are the best candidate for the job. Topics always come to me right when I leave an interview or get off the phone. These are perfect for the thank you note because they act as an added bonus about yourself. Wait a few hours to see if some ideas begin to stir, but always send the note the same day as the interview.

Chapter 5

Restaurant Careers

Variety: One of the biggest pros of working in a restaurant is variation. You end up learning about several regions, styles and producers every shift and usually without realizing it. Think about the difference for a moment: You work for a winery or a brand, guess what you learn about and/or speak about every day? That brand, that winery. Also, you'd better make damn sure that you're extremely passionate about those wines or that company. Being said, working in a restaurant is one of the best places to learn about all types of wine, as well as spirits, beer and more. I truly believe that anyone interested in wine should work in a restaurant at least once, for the mere reason variety and exposure.

Your Hours: Well, you can sleep in pretty much every day, as most people (especially Americans) mainly drink wine in the evenings. Your nights however, can be very late. Sure, you'll have a random dead shift and go home early, but you won't know when that's going to be. This means that planning dinner with friends has to be a last-minute process. As you climb the FOH (front of house) ladder, your days and nights could mold into a more ideal schedule for you. However, since the drinking usually takes place at night, the best wine orders do too. Sommeliers, Wine Runners, and Beverage Directors need to be around in the evenings.

A Passion for Service: I'll admit, I'm a very impatient person. In my world, there's literally nothing worse than bad service. Many servers and Sommeliers consider themselves professionals and take as much pride in perfecting the guest experience as they do in learning about wine. Failing to meet the guests' expectations is taken very seriously. If you remember that their happiness comes before that of any manager or restaurant owner, you will succeed in the restaurant business. From dive to white tablecloth, intense to super casual, service will absolutely make or break your success. To quote Danny Meyer, "You don't go to the trattoria with the best pasta, you go to the trattoria that loves you the most."

The Server

Servers are one of the most important pieces to a successful restaurant pie. An exceptional, wine-knowledgeable server can likely advance to a Sommelier, Captain or Manager very quickly. Service Captains may hold the keys for closing and opening, count the tips at the end of the night, and even manage the servers. Usually the Captain(s) have several wine-focused responsibilities as well. It's important to note that a serving position at a renowned restaurant can be more substantial for education and growth than a Sommelier or Wine Director of a lesser known establishment.

Take Eleven Madison Park for example. This award-winning restaurant requires every employee to start at the Assistant Server position, no matter their wine experience or certifications. This is part of their rigorous training program and benefits both the new hire as well as management. The new employees learn every step that goes into the service system, from the kitchen to the table. Some people take weeks to get to their desired position, some years, and some even find that they enjoy something else along the way.

Contrary to what you may believe, service can be tricky. When I first started out, I forgot orders, accidentally spilled a bowl of pasta down someone's back, and even broke a mirror with a flying Champagne cork. It isn't rocket science but it does take time and patience. The only bad servers are the ones who absolutely *don't care*. Not only can *WE* easily point them out, restaurant owners and managers especially can. If you're brand new and eager to learn, you're already better than the half that wish they were doing something else.

Serving advice:

- Pay attention to the details! Hot sauce on the side, a side of beets without beet juice, just do it.

- Write down all of your orders! It just makes things easier, you don't have to guess that they want their Manhattan up and not on the rocks. Plus, you might be distracted by another table on your way to typing in the order.

- Be responsible for other sections too. If you see an issue at another table, and their server is busy, get over there. This holds especially true if your restaurant is on a "shared tip-pool" system. Also, helping others is cool.

- Don't leave empty glasses or plates on the table, it screams amateur and it's also nasty.

- Don't gossip, you never know who has super-hearing or lip-reading capabilities.

- If you have to use your cell phone, do it in the bathroom or on a break. It just says that you don't care about watching over your tables.

The Assistant Sommelier

Also known as a Wine Runner, this position is perfect for a wine-studious Server, eventually interested in a Sommelier position. While a large portion of your week might involve unloading cases of wine, and sticker-ing bottles for inventory, you will likely be invited to taste with reps. Tastings are inarguably the best way to learn about wine, in fact it's the only way to process quality. Most of us are hands-on learners and studying words and maps can only get us so far. How else could you fully understand acidity, tannin, or body without tasting?

Assistant Somms are also relied upon when stepping in for the Sommelier(s) when they are off the floor and/or too busy to get to the table. They take wine orders, pour tableside, decant, and much more. Depending on the establishment, advancing to the Sommelier title might actually be dependent upon passing your Certified with the Court. Before then, I recommend volunteering yourself around the establishment, and practicing bottle and champagne opening at home. The best advice I have for Assistant Somms: prove that you're serious and really care about the restaurant and wine program. Come in hours before your shift to help out if they need it, and wine focused restaurants usually do.

The Sommelier

In most cases, you can be considered for this position after a few years as a server or assistant Somm. You will likely be ordering with the Wine Director (who might also be the owner or manager). You will also be invited to several tastings, as well as make appointments with your sales reps. On a daily basis, you will taste wines in which you and/or the Wine Director are interested in ordering. Unlike serving, Sommeliers are responsible for opening bottles and pouring glasses of wine. They seldom drop food or take food orders. This is by far the best position for tasting and learning about wine. It is (or should be) a duty to taste each bottle that's ordered, making sure it isn't corked, maderized, or faulty in some other way. As mentioned, tasting faults requires much practice, but it is very important when considering the guest experience and the restaurant's reputation.

The formality of a Sommelier depends entirely on the restaurant. From laid-back atmospheres that don't even use a trays to full-on French service, I can't tell you exactly what processes you will need to learn. No matter the restaurant, I'm a fan of always pouring tastes. This not only includes bottle orders, but glass orders as well. This allows the guest to try a couple of wines before deciding on their favorite. It makes them feel special, and proven to increase how many glasses they order.

Training the servers and staff is another important duty of this position. The wait staff didn't order the wines on the list, so it's your job to tell them why you and/or the Wine Director did. Restaurants that are focused on wine and food education are truly the best to work for. In my experience, establishments with the greatest retention have a "casual with high standards" style.

You'll also find yourself using software daily, which will help you majorly. For example, Binwise (for creating wine lists and keeping accurate inventory) and SevenFifty (for ordering wines from your distributors, creating tasting sheets, and much more). The training is minimal, but keep in mind that some computer skills are required.

Event Sommeliers

The role of an Event Sommelier can be taken as either easier or more difficult than a typical restaurant Sommelier. This is completely dependent upon your personality. Working events, you're never surprised by the "the 10:30 10-top" you'd find weekly in restaurants. Surprise, late-night diners can be stressful, annoying, and impossible to plan your week around.

On the other hand, Event Servers and Somms have to deal with some pretty intense personalities. We're talking crazy planners, bride and/or groom-zillas, mother of the bride and/or (but usually) mother of the groom-zillas, CHILDREN, drunken bachelorette parties, ridiculous requests, the list goes on. The best part about working as an Event Somm is knowing exactly when you're getting off work. This holds especially true for those who require an organized and structured calendar. Also, you will likely have every detail beforehand, with plenty of time to plan for impeccable service.

The only downfall is that you need to find an establishment with regular events, so that your pay is stable. Then again, working "on call" can be a great option for someone with another job that's interested in extra income.

Wine Directors and Buyers

Before getting into one of the most sought after wine careers, I have a short example of the importance of this role. Last year, a fellow Sommelier and I decided to try a new spot in the Lower East Side, known for their wine list. With only 10 food items, I was shocked to see an 8 page wine list, but hey, maybe that works for them. Per usual, we wanted to try as many different wines that the evening would allow. So, we decided to order different glasses throughout the night, rather than splitting a bottle.

I told her to choose first, and after almost a minute (way too long) she asked, "What's Counoise?" I explained the Rhone origin and what it tastes like. Wait what? They have Counoise by the glass? And actually listed the grape? That's odd. Moving on, we both read this list and gave each other weird looks several times. I couldn't believe that *we* were having such difficulty ordering a glass of wine. Finally, the server arrived to take our wine order. I said, "So, what's Adoracca?" He rolled his eyes and I could tell this wasn't the first time he's heard this question. He wasn't coming off rude, just annoyed at his Wine Director's decisions. If we were asking him that, just imagine who else was confused out of their minds, looking for anything remotely recognizable. This restaurant is no longer in business and I believe that there is a time and place to be creative with your wine list. At the end of the day, figure out if your small restaurant should keep the weird stuff to a minimum or label it differently. Instead of Adoracca, how about "Calabrian dry white" Your customers *and* your staff will undoubtedly thank you.

Let's talk about placing orders. Once you've found a few distributors you would like to work with, it's time to place some orders. You can choose to work with five or twenty-five, that part's up to you. Although, the more distributors you have, the more confusing payments and wine drops can be. You could probably cover even a large wine list by only ordering through four to seven companies.

Also, keep in mind that it is pretty rude to taste with a rep you have no interest in ordering from. Even if you're studying and should taste to learn about varietals, stick with the people you already work with. Try putting yourself in the rep's shoes and definitely read the upcoming chapter on careers in wholesale. Your rep probably drove to you, put in sample requests for you, and is counting on your order (among others) to pay his rent this month. Come on, most of these guys and gals work solely on commission.

Being in charge of the wine list as the Beverage Director is the ultimate goal of many Sommeliers and restaurant owners. This is honestly a blast, as you have a chance to be creative and speak about your passions on a daily basis. You can either have a strict plan for when and what to order, or just buy what you like and fill "list holes" as they come. It's about finding your style and defining who you are, which you may find changes monthly (along with your palate).

The best Wine Directors understand the importance of having options, while realizing trends and past desires of the guests. Many diners enjoy classic styles of wine, while some prefer to taste something new from somewhere new, every time they go out. An ever-changing list is always fun, but you have to buy what sells, right? Also, keep the wine list in line with the food! Wines with new oak and/or high alcohol hardly work with most food items, but people sure tend to like them. So, have one option, not ten, or your food might end up tasting like nothing at all. Also, most people drink what they want and eat what they want, without giving a crap about how they taste together. A nice balance is important, but I'd encourage your staff to always help the guest pair their meal.

In all honesty, many Bev directors work 10am 'til midnight. They need to be around during lunch and dinner service, floating around the tables and chatting about wine. When it's slow, they can check email, stock wine and place orders. There can be a glamorous facade attached to this position, as they're in the spotlight and tend to get a lot of attention. Wine Directors are never surprised to hear their name whispered while walking around the restaurant. Major egos exist for this reason, and some of them even act like celebrities. Eye-roll.

I know a Wine Director in particular who hides around the corners of his restaurant, as if there are paparazzi or a few screaming fans. I've seen people ask to meet him and then observe as he whispers to his Sommelier to tell them he's busy or not in. Isn't the whole point of this job about creating the best possible guest experience? A wine chat with the Head Somm or Wine Director would definitely encourage a customer to come back. That's a memorable moment! For the most part, however, they're passionate dorks who unload cases of wine all day.

As far as income goes, you will either be given a steady salary or a few more "points." The point system in a restaurant is based on the responsibilities of the staff, allowing those with more required duties to receive more of the tip pool. Another potential positive is that all of this ordering may allow you to leave the floor altogether. Therefore, you can strictly work in the office, placing orders and dealing with wine ordering issues that arise. Most who hold this office-style Wine Director position still need to be there throughout the evenings, just in case they need to present a bottle to a VIP, or deal with a dining issue. If you are considering this position, I hope you love to be a mentor because plenty of servers and sommeliers depend on learning from you. Second, realize now that wine should be welcoming, not alienating.

The Manager

As you probably know or expect, Managers are not necessarily wine focused, but depending on the size of the restaurant, they can be. Managers are usually responsible for the staff; training, hiring, firing and scheduling. Managers can make significantly more than servers and sommeliers, as well as have more attractive work schedules. I would seriously consider this position if you are great with people and fine with less of a wine focus. Again, this depends on the size of the business and some managers also purchase and present wine. Most times however, managers are usually concerned with ordering the forks, calling the plumber, and screwing in the lightbulbs. Keep in mind that in some cases, especially small restaurants, the manager and Wine Director is the same person.

The Restaurant Owner

Owning an establishment could mean doing everything or nothing at all. I will say that restaurants can be hard to not only keep alive, but to be profitable. You obviously need a good idea, a location that makes sense, and an all-around need from the community. I would make sure that you are ready to make this your "baby." You will likely be there every day, making several decisions. Being said, leaving town for the weekend might be out of the question, for a while at least.

I always say that a successful restaurant is a place that you really want to spend time in and a place you love to take your friends. Sometimes being there 12 hours a day, especially upon first opening, is the best thing for yourself and everyone else. If you haven't been open long, how do you know the right number of servers per time of day, or what your customer *really* wants? Some owners have one idea of a restaurant, and then figure out that it doesn't meet any needs of the neighborhood. They can either change things accordingly or pray that everyone in town will get on board with their idea.

Like managers, owners are often the ones dealing with the less-exciting stuff like liquor licenses, paying rent, and passing inspections. If you have a great idea and see a true need, by all means, find a book on restaurant ownership and pursue this.

Chapter 6

Retail Careers

Unlike working in restaurants, those with careers in retail have a very consistent schedule. Similar to restaurants however, an inviting and confident attitude is extremely important. You will be regularly exploring all wines of the world, so an open mind is very much required.

Sales and Consulting

Shop Girl (or Boy): Some people absolutely love this position, others would rather break a wine bottle over their head. Here's my reasoning for the latter, more violent approach: When you're not unloading wine and dusting bottles, you're helping customers find what they are looking for. Helping people is the job, but it can be extremely repetitive and annoying at times. You may find yourself keeping a tally in your notebook titled, "# of times I've shown a woman a bottle of cheap Pinot Grigio today."

Now for the positives: You'll probably work noon to 8pm, with very little stress in your day to day activities. If you aren't the one ordering the wine, late deliveries and bounced checks aren't your problem. You will likely have a less-than-impressive hourly pay. Of course that can be stressful, but just when you're trying to pay rent and not while you're there. Commission won't likely go into effect until a year or two of working and gaining a client list. Another positive: you get to taste wine all the time. How else would you be able to sell it? Plus, fat wine discounts can save you majorly, especially if you're studying and new to the industry.

All said, happiness in this position is very dependent upon the manager and/or owner of the shop. If he or she is a happy person and offers you decent pay, you'll be alright. This is a great place to start, as you can easily learn and study wine throughout the day. I actually completed an entire online wine course while working as a Shop Girl.

The Wine Consultant: This can be one of the best and most financially rewarding jobs in wine, that is if you have (or are given) a substantial list of clients. What do I mean by CLIENTS? Take that list of people who buy wine from you, then remove the ones who don't purchase on a monthly basis. Example: Suzanne buys a bottle of $200 Champagne for her boss the week before Christmas. Remove Suzanne.

Let's say you have no list, or a very small one... what do you do? Anything you can think of! Networking, social media, volunteer at a local golf tournament, hang out with your uncle at the country club. I think you catch my drift. As much as it sucks, the $12 Pinot Grigio ladies you met as a Shop Girl aren't going to make a dent in your annual sales goal. When you're working the shop, be on the lookout for people who do qualify as a real consulting client. Get their email address, phone number and preferences if you can. If you let them leave without getting their info, you could be missing out on a serious client. Then, care about them! Help them find exactly what they might want, when they come in or not, based on their preferences and your conversations.

As a consultant, it is extremely important to email your clients about wines that make sense to them, based on their purchase history. If you send everyone an offer on California Chardonnay and half of them hate the stuff, you're bound to lose a few clients. I recommend Mailchimp for e-blasting, as you can track who opens and clicks very easily, targeting them for other wine offers, phone-call follow ups, and more. There are so many great email marketing software systems out there and they all do basically the same thing. I also recommend SailThru, but it takes a while to figure it out as there's a bit of coding involved. Some pick this up easier than others, but in the end, the offers look great and they are easy to personalize. For example, you can add the person's name to the e-blast to make it look like you are only sending the offer to them. Also, you can send it at the time the person is most likely to read their emails. Oh, technology!

If you don't have a client book, hopefully you can ease your way into the store's commission structure. Some shops I've worked for clearly understand this, others really don't care and have a "you make when I make" mentality. It's a shame to see great people have to leave their job just because they're new. While I don't know your current financial situation, commission based positions can be extremely difficult in the beginning. If paying your rent is going to be questionable as you begin your career as a wine consultant, consider having another job to start. Perhaps you'll find that consulting part-time, while working another job is best for security reasons.

My dear friend, Jesse Warner-Levine was a Wine Consultant for a luxury retailer for almost a decade and now he is opening a shop of his own. Check out his take on the career of a consultant.

---

1. *After realizing that wine was your passion, what made you decide to get into the retail side? Can you tell me about a few other things you tried that got you to that conclusion?*

"I can't say that I realized my passion and then decided to enter retail. Rather I ended up in wine retail, and then realized my passion. That's what is so awesome about working in this industry. As your knowledge grows, so does the joy of working in wine. Wine encompasses history, geology, geography, weather, war, tradition, superstition, travel, food, and lifestyle. When it comes right down to it, it's all about tying on a proper buzz. I worked in restaurants throughout high school and college, then tried wholesale in Ohio and NY, and now retail for nearly a decade. It sounds silly, but I was simply too sweaty to carry a wine bag around NYC.

I'm lucky, retail has worked out in my favor. For starters, I learned what I was doing wrong on the wholesale side. Understanding what the customer needs is the most important aspect to any sales job. I found that the retail customer is interested in learning about wine in a nonpretentious way, which I always prefer. Working in a wine shop also gave me the opportunity to develop my own opinion about wine. Unlike wholesale, in retail you're not required to keep your allegiance to a certain collection. If you're a wholesaler you need to believe in your portfolio fully. In retail you're allowed to change your mind. If I buy 72 bottles of something and if you discover it sucks, I put it on sale, sell it, and move on to pick something else.

It was also necessary for me to learn more, and by doing so my confidence increased. Retail allowed me the time to learn and my customer base grew as I grew. Working in wholesale in NYC just made me feel intimidated."

2. *When you first started and had a small (or nonexistent) book of clients, how did you best grow that book? What advice do you have for someone just starting out?*

"If you have a small book of retail clients you need to FOLLOW UP! You also need to ask for referrals. Keep it personal! Don't rely on social media or CRM platforms in trade for personal relationships. All email correspondence, offers, phone calls, texts need to be crafted in a manner that has one specific person in mind. One offer goes to one single person. If the customer can feel that you're acting on their behalf, they'll buy. They'll even pay more. Be honest, people notice and will create loyalty. If you get a feeling like you're being too "sales-y" then you're doing it wrong. You're building a relationship not a fast buck."

3. *Biggest struggles as a consultant? And best perks?*

"For me its organization and the allocation of time, I futz around preparing for questions that never come. I'm sure that's just being professional but you just need to get the work done. The best perk is when you're job is going well. If I'm doing my job perfectly, I'm only doing the fun parts. I sit with people, drink great wine and create relationships. That's the job.

4. *I hear you're opening your own wine shop! Can you tell me why you've decided to go that route?*

"I'm currently in the thick of development at Convive Wine & Spirits. We're opening in the East Village. What started as a summer open will most definitely be fall, so my outlook on WHY is a bit strange. The experience thus far has been painful slowdowns, stop work orders and way more expenses than I thought were possible. I'm also acutely aware that my business partner, Blue and I haven't even gotten to the hard part of actually running the business. Couple that with the chance that I might not know what I'm doing and you understand my stress.

The flip side is that there is a chance at real success or at the very least, a livable wage. I feel that the bar of service in wine retail is low. Stores may have a good website but have bad customer service, or a nice store but they don't track specific customer buying habits. We're also implementing a direct-to-consumer salesforce, attempting to offer one "wine guy" for every possible customer. I've never had the opportunity to think about the big picture and I'm the perfect mix of excited and terrified." –Jesse Warner Levine, Owner, Convive Wine and Spirits

Buyers

Nine out of ten wine buyers do a whole lot more than just buy, they're managers, owners, and salespeople. However, I worked at a wine store where the buyer came in twice per week, between 8:00am and noon. He was a stay-at-home dad, and even came in with both kids before the doors opened. Based on his schedule, you can probably gather that he never properly bought anything. He wasn't checking any sales reports and had no idea what was out of stock or needed for upcoming seasons and events. Buyers should have the freedom to buy because they know, study and speak with their customers on a daily basis.

So what should shops always keep in stock? Of course that depends on many factors, but I would say that keeping a variety of the most popular grapes is best. I didn't say most popular producers, because that depends on what your customers are asking for. After hearing "Do you have any Whispering Angel?" seven times, I found the source and ordered it. It wasn't my absolute favorite, but it met the customers' needs and I sold cases of it.

I would advise any buyer to look at sales reports and keep your prices in line with the clientele. The big spenders are likely going to come in and ask for something random that doesn't make sense for your store. Here's where special ordering comes in. In New York, most distribution companies have a minimum order of 3 cases for next-day delivery. Not bad, especially if you know that you can sell the wine to local (preferably a few) regular spending clients. Ask your client if he or she would like a few cases, as this is a great opportunity to make a big sale. If not, purchase the minimum amount, but only if you see another opportunity to sell the rest. Maybe this wine would make sense for another client you have in mind. Perhaps this is your chance to keep a high-roller client happily ordering from you forever. See how buying and consulting are usually the responsibilities of just one person now?

Don't place all of your orders at once and don't only order the wine you like. I learned this in my adult industry days, when I got to order the Halloween costumes for fall. I looked through all the catalogs, found my favorites, and guess what? Nothing sold. I thought for sure the Slutty Astronaut and Sexy Snow Angel would be a creative hit amongst our audience. It turned out to be another year of the French Maid and Sexy Cop. Our clientele just wasn't ready for these creative styles, and we took a hit because they wouldn't sell the following year either. The moral of my story is to be careful filling the shelves with $300 Riesling when your customers drink $20 Cab. The bottles will not only collect dust, they may turn faulty (if not stored correctly) before someone ends up buying them. When they finally do, that'll be the last of your high-end Riesling customer.

Next, if you're gonna geek out, be careful. You'll quickly find that California Mouverdre, while interesting and delicious, is probably going to sit on your shelf longer than the $300 Riesling. I've seen it too many times with new wine shop owners, an entire section dedicated to "interesting" wine. Necessary? Probably not. Then again, your shop might be next door to a wine school and your post-class walk-in customers are nerdier than you are.

Successful purchasing takes time. Look at your sales, talk to your customers, and lastly, consider labels. Some people love a traditional label, maybe it reminds them of their trip to Italy in the 90s. Others like a loud, colorful and possibly funny, modern label. I like to have a good mix of both to start, and notice where the eyes and dollars go. This will likely be based on your neighborhood and age demographic. Restaurants don't have this problem, as most diners will find their favorite style, the first wine in their budget, or the first one they can easily pronounce without ever seeing the label.

Purchasing Collections (Auction and Consignment): Buying cellars on consignment or for auction is either boring or interesting, you have to decide that for yourself. First, you really have to know what you're doing. You need to have extensive knowledge about regions, producers and vintages, as each factor can increase or decrease the number you decide to put on the bottle. You'll also base this number on professional scores, which you'll need to check daily. While I'm not filling my cellar based on what Uncle Bob (Robert Parker) has to say, many people sure do. They find a critic they like and they're a slave to the scores. Somebody had to rate it, and I'm not complaining because it makes assessments a whole lot easier for me. We also have sites like Winesearcher.com and Winemarketjournal. com that can quickly and easily display which wines sold where, for what, and when. However, uploading a collector's wine can be quite tedious and again, you have to know your wine.

Let's say Mr. Burnett sends you a list of his collection. Maybe he sent a written note via his office fax machine, maybe it's in Microsoft Word or even better, Microsoft Excel and you can import it. Once, a client sent me his list via text images written on cocktail napkins. In any case, you might be getting partial information on the wine you need to identify. I've had collectors abbreviate names (probably in an attempt to be cool), or send lists of wines that completely contradict themselves, "Joseph Phelps Napa Pinot Chard from Sonoma Coast."

Also, some of these people just don't understand the valuations. They figured they bought great wine in great vintages and it can only be five times the price they paid now, right? Very wrong. I can't tell you how many times I've had to break the news that entire collections are worth half of what they paid and now everything's over the hill. You have to watch your wine, use the internet, talk to consultants, and figure out what you should finally open this Thanksgiving. Don't be a wine hoarder.

When you have a great collection and you're ready to purchase, it's time to inspect. Obviously, you can't re-sell a bottle of wine that looks like it's been to hell and back. The cosmetic appearance means a lot to the new buyer. Examples: cork popping upward or downward from where it should be, missing pieces of labels or ones with weird stains, and the most common: fill levels. Aged wine that hasn't been stored properly might look like somebody siphoned a glass out of it. Wine *does* naturally grace downward after several years in the bottle, but people do not like to buy ¾ of a bottle for the price of the whole thing. It can be a little intimidating letting a collector know that you can't accept some of their wines. This is just part of the job, and honestly most fine wine collectors understand this.

Owning and Managing a Wine Store

Like restaurants, find out if the neighborhood even needs another store. How near and similar are the closest wine shops? In most states, you must be a specified distance away from the 3 closest shops. This makes perfect sense to me. Why would there be a *need* for another shop if 4 are already on the same block? So, before you go whining about how dated these "prohibition-era" regulations are, the state might actually be doing you a favor. If you *do* see a need for a physical store in a certain area of your town, check out your competition. How are they doing? Do they seem busy, or have the same wines been sitting on the shelf since last season?

Once you find the right neighborhood, fully consider the retail spaces for rent. Are you on a side-street with no traffic, or a busy, two-way street with more residences than offices? Location is practically everything. I often find myself shopping at the not-so-great liquor store, solely out of convenience and proximity to my house. Yes, I give recommendations every time I shop.

Wine shop managers are usually selling and buying the wine in the store. Unlike restaurants, retail managers have more involvement with the wine, but it still may not compare to the time spent on managing. They are supervising and scheduling employees and dealing with various store issues. Much like owning and managing a restaurant, you better love to be there all the time, nurturing your little baby.

I've also found the best wine shop owners are chill, knowledgeable and fair. If you're looking to own a shop, please pay your staff appropriately and try to offer some type of benefits. If you don't offer fair pay, the best people will just keep leaving. Too small to offer benefits? Three weeks of vacation, even if only during the two slowest months, could ultimately result in an employee for life. When hiring, look for the ones with the most passion and drive. Invite them to tastings, listen to their ideas, and treat them with respect.

Chapter 7

Wholesale Careers

The Office Managers and Assistants

I don't know anyone who *loves* their job as an Office Manager in a distribution office, but it's a fantastic place to start. First of all, an abundance of wine knowledge is hardly necessary. You're pulling samples, so label recognition is a plus but can also be memorized. Other than that, you're taking inventory or putting orders in for the sales team. This is a great place for a studious newcomer, as you'll likely be able to taste with the reps before they leave the office for appointments.

As a rep, I opened my samples in the office to make sure they weren't corked, and I would always ask my office crew if they wanted to taste. This also had to do with the fact that a full bottle is heavier than half a bottle. A half bottle also makes you look busier to the buyers at your appointments. Most of the time, I would dump half the bottle down the drain to reduce the weight of my bag. This was especially the case after a couple of slipped disks in my back. Sorry, Wine Gods.

This position requires organization and sometimes you have to be very firm with the sales team. Maybe they tried to order a wine that's now out of stock and you need to call them and tell them, "You should have read the current price book." I've actually seen a few sales reps end up in this position because the commission structure (or stress to sell) wasn't in line with their desirable and stable life.

Sales Reps

If you don't have a car and/or don't like driving, think long and hard before going down this path. Are you physically willing and able to wheel or carry wine around all day without a car? It might be heavier and more uncomfortable than you think. Alas, everyone's bodies and strengths are completely different, and I'm only warning the car-less that they had better be in shape. For me, working for a small importer in NYC meant Brooklyn and back 4 times per day by subway. You may not realize how many staircases that is right now, but you would with 4-9 bottles in your wine bag. Shoulder-bag or wheeler, if you can't bench 220 on the reg, you are royally screwed without a car.

If you do have a car or love walking around with a heavy wine bag, working for a distributor or importer can be immensely rewarding and quite flexible. First, you can practically make your own schedule, usually booking your own appointments whenever you feel like. Even better, restaurants won't see you after their "pre-shift meeting" (this is the staff meal and usually around 4 or 5pm). Retail stores also get very busy around 5pm and won't take appointments when they are trying to sell wine. Cooking at home and Happy Hours with friends are exceptionally feasible, especially in comparison to restaurant and retail careers.

One of the biggest difficulties in this position is gaining enough regular spending accounts. You may be thinking, "But I'm a hot chick, can't I just use my sex appeal??" I don't know how hot you are, but from my experience, it's not that easy. Sure, they'll taste with you, but guess who they'll regularly place their orders with? Their bros! The ones they go on family vacations with. As a *younger* woman, I would often get the feeling that the owners and buyers were thinking, "I'm not gonna listen to a word you have to say because last night I drank a bottle of wine that's older than you." Some folks don't think you can possibly show them something they don't already know, especially not at *your* age.

On the positive side, you'll meet some real characters and hear some crazy stories that make your day. Meet my favorite account, an old steakhouse in the heart of the Financial District. Now, meet the owner and buyer, Carratto. Envision a large Italian man, about 65 years old with the thickest New York Accent you've ever heard and a napkin hanging down the front of his shirt. Carratto only wanted to buy wine during his restaurant's "family meal." Now I'm not sure if you've worked in a restaurant, but family meals usually consist of penne, some greens, and whatever left-over meat that's listed to go bad the following day. Carratto's however, involved fresh lobster, filet mignon, potatoes au gratin, oysters(!), and pretty much the priciest stuff you can eat.

The first time I met him, he told me that I looked just like a hooker he met in Atlantic City. "Big eyes, bright red hair, coulda been ya twin, honey." Per his request, I'd stop in between 4:30pm and 5:30pm, Monday or Friday, no appointment necessary. He'd force me to "eat somethin'!" and I'd show him the wines in my bag, as long as they were Italian and Steak-house approved. But NEVER, I mean NEVER would he call, text or email *me* the order. He'd call Jon, the owner of the business to place his orders. Sexist? Maybe. I took it as macho and I really didn't care. I figured he just wanted to make sure his boy knew he was loyal. Either way, I didn't care, his stories and the entertainment was just too good. I ended up showing him wine every week to hear his stories. "Couple guys come in, wipe out all my Tuscans, know what I'm sayin'? Then, one of em passes out on the floor. It aint even noon and I says to the guy, 'Getthefuckoutaheaaa!'" As you might not be so lucky to get a real gem like Caratto, you'll likely meet some characters in this industry that make you smile. Be open to working around their schedules, because they will appreciate it and probably give you a sympathy sale.

Also, don't waste your time tasting with the non-buyer, at least not more than a few times. They can't make any decisions and will rarely tell the real buyer about their afternoon tasting with you. A wine's structure and tasting notes can be difficult to explain to someone else anyway, since our palates are all so different. Be a shark and call, email, and drop by for the owner or buyer ONLY. As mentioned in previous chapters, this is usually the same person.

The day-to-day of this job is quite enjoyable, especially if you don't mind sitting at the bar of restaurants, eating and drinking on your company's dime. This is called the "walk-in" and your job is to schmooze with the bartender, figure out the owner/buyer's name and leave your "book" (Pricelist). The problem with "the book" is that it gets thrown in the trash 9 out of 10 times. I hate wasting paper, especially 15 pages each walk-in. Instead, I'd figure out their "list holes" and recommend something in their price point that falls in line with the theme of the place. Then, I'd write it on the back of one of my single page "tasting sheets." With every appointment, you print a tasting sheet so that the buyer(s) can follow along, view prices, discounts on purchasing more than one case, etc. Also, the tasting sheet has your email and phone number in the upper left hand corner, making it larger and perhaps more save-worthy than a dinky business card.

This is a pretty slow-pace job and the only time you'll need to really hustle is when you're killing it or trying to get all of your orders in on Thursday afternoon. Restaurants and shops need their Friday drops before the weekend, when trucks don't deliver. The real stress of this job lies within making sales. I often get asked about commission structures and average pay for importer/distributor jobs, and there's really not one easy answer. This completely depends on the company you work for, how many clients will be given to you, how many you come in with, how good you are at sales, and how long your training base will occur.

I am most fond of a "progressive system." I think that more companies should give their salespeople a chance to gain clients. They should have the data and experience to know how long this takes. Honestly, it takes about a year for someone without a book of clients. So how about a base for the first 4 months, half base and half commission for 8, and then full commission (which you may actually want) at the 12 month mark? Some companies would be into this, some are less patient. Remember that the time of year has a lot to do with your sales success. The summers in New York City are notoriously slow, as everyone goes out of town. Seasonally speaking, on heavily commission-based pay structures, you better save and plan for it. Get in with that local beirgarten! Show them your rosé with the fattest quantity in April and they'll need to re-order it all summer long.

Be picky when finding a company to work for. You can look at their wine portfolio online to get a sense of who they are and who their clients are. For instance, you find a company that sells very inexpensive wine. That probably means that your clients will be lower-end businesses and you will only be tasting and learning about inexpensive wine. Does that matter to you? What about large companies, are they better or worse? That depends. They will probably have benefits and a fair commission structure, but which territory are they trying to fill? It may be the one that nobody wants. Also, a well-known company can have a good or bad reputation. Your clients either know and trust the company, or they might have had a bad experience in the past.

How about brand new companies? Well, you'll probably be able to choose your own territory, if you even have one. In smaller companies, the whole city might be fair game. However, no one will know of you when you introduce yourself and may conclude that's because the company hasn't been worth knowing. Many restaurant and wine shop owners think they know everything and everyone. Hopefully they're not too proud to admit they don't know your company and proceed to give you a chance. New companies rarely have the means to offer benefits or a decent commission structure. These are love projects, started by seasoned wine professionals.

Most of these guys are selling as well, reaching out to all of their industry connections in order to pay their own salary.

Be perceptive to the company culture upon interviewing. Does everyone seem happy and relatively organized? I interviewed with an all-Italian importer once and felt a very drab vibe in the office. Later that day, the owner had an offer for me, and I came to read that they didn't give new hires a base salary *at all*. I also found out that they made their employees pay for their own wine samples. Seriously? These are just a few things to keep in mind when finding the right company to work for.

Big positive: get ready to never pay for another bottle of wine again! You'll be sure to come home with the day's leftover samples (usually 5 or so half-full bottles). I've found this great for tastings with peers, study groups, or just a good time. This sector of the industry is arguably the best, because you get to have interesting conversations about wine with people who share your passion.

Above restaurant and retail careers, the importance of the company you work for falls the highest. Among my peers, I've literally heard it all. If they have Craigslist listings every week, that's probably a bad sign. One of my very good friends who works for a phenomenal distributor in New York City has offered to share her experience below. She decided to stay anonymous.

1. **Has working for a wine distribution company gone exactly how you imagined it? If not, what were some surprises or struggles?**

"A big misunderstanding that people often have (and that I had early on) about being a rep is just how hard it is to get established. Sometimes if you are seasoned rep with a good reputation it's possible to be hired and handed an active account list, but typically (and especially if you are new to selling) you start with a list of dead accounts or nothing at all, which is very challenging. Countless contacts of mine from restaurants and retail have made the move to become a sales rep and almost all of them quit and almost immediately.

It takes an incredible amount of effort and time to establish an account list. You face a lot of rejection and if you are the kind person who is likely to take rejection personally then this is definitely not the right line of work for you.

The first year is tough and you make almost no money. You are usually on a draw for the first six months (which you negotiate with the company), but it's usually nothing to write home about. Typically, it's not until 1.5-2 years in that you are making a good salary."

2. **What can you tell me about the company you work for that I can't find online? Anything (good or bad) that wasn't expected or differs from other companies?**

"It's the best importer/distributor you can work for. Hands down. I would never even dream of working for another distributor as a sales rep. David really takes care of his employees and he treats everyone that works for him like family- no matter how long they have been there or what position they hold. Also, another plus: the benefits are comparable to a larger company--with 401k matching and 100% health insurance paid. Most people who work here have been here 5-13 years (the company is 13 years old). And with a company of 30+ people that says a lot I think.

One way that Bowler is a bit different than other companies is that there are never any sales quotas. But you are expected to continually grow your sales, of course. We are 100% commission based. We don't have sample budgets (most companies give each rep a certain amount of money per month for samples). Our office is in NYC's Flatiron, so you can come into the office to pick up samples, work out of the office at any time and hold meetings with buyers in the conference rooms. We each attend at least one wine trip per year."

3. **What would you tell someone who just got certified and wants to be a sales rep for a distribution company? Your advice, opinions, regrets, etc..**

"I don't think you need to be certified. In fact, maybe one or two salesperson at Bowler are. A genuine curiosity for wine knowledge is all that's required. You learn so much in this line of work: everyday appointments with buyers, travel, working the market with winemakers and portfolio tastings. The knowledge will come organically if you have the interest.

While basic wine knowledge is essential, I think what's almost more important is being comfortable with rejection. You also have to be self-motivated, persistent, organized and good at building relationships. And you have to be good at asking for what you want and having frank conversations.

Even if you have all of the right qualifications to be a rep, it's absolutely essential to work for a good company that has strong manager/director/office staff support systems. Even after seven years of doing this job, I call our Sales Director and VP all the time to bounce ideas off of them or just vent. I think it's important to have that if you want to continue growing.

A few other things I've heard from friends at other companies:

Working for a company where the owner/partner is also selling wine usually leaves the other sales reps at a disadvantage in terms of getting top or new accounts and allocated or limited items.

Also, if you are a woman that is planning to have a family one day: Many other distributors have terrible or non-existent maternity leave policies. If you plan on having a family, it doesn't hurt to ask around about a company's policy."

Buying for Importing and/ or Distribution Companies

The role of a wine buyer depends on the size of the company. In the case of small companies, the owner usually does this because it's the best part! They literally travel around the world (or whatever regions they specialize in), tasting wine and buying their favorites. Larger companies may hire a team of buyers to travel, taste wine, and find those secret little gems who haven't been discovered. That requires some serious trust from the owner, as well as a seasoned palate, both of which can take many years to develop.

Keep in mind that Importers have an abundance of logistics to deal with. From each country's laws and taxation to every Bill of Lading, this position requires attention to detail and reading through what seems to be endless paperwork. You should also be able to speak the languages of the countries you are purchasing from. This could mean taking a language course. Keep in mind that larger companies have specific buying positions and working for smaller companies requires wearing many hats.

Chapter 8

Winery Careers

The Tasting Room Tender

So you live somewhere that makes wine? Beautiful! This is a good one, as long as drunken bachelorette parties don't bother you. Not all wineries allow walk-ins, or parties larger than 6, but most do. This position involves lots of standing, pouring and talking, much like teaching, which you will hear about later.

The Tasting Room Tender is much like a Wine Shop Girl or Boy, if there were only one producer in the store. He or she speaks about the estate, each wine, and the winemaking process in a quick and simple fashion. Usually, however, they do much more. Some weekly tasks include: pulling wines for orders, cleaning and organizing the tasting room, sales and retention, wine club assistance, and more.

The Winery Manager

Even more hats to wear here. The Winery Manager's job is to manage employees, gain new business and increase wine sales. However, you may find that they assist the Winemaker and Assistant Winemaker on a daily basis. Types of duties will usually depend on the size of the winery. The manager may also be the Tasting Room Tender, or even act as a liaison between the winery and the sales people representing the brand.

Like any manager, there are several non-wine responsibilities that involve having a high tolerance for people. Managers assist in the hiring and scheduling, and like restaurant and retail, there may be less of a wine focus. My sister-in-law, Breanna has been a very successful manager at her father's winery for over a decade in Sonoma, California. She's offered to answer a few questions about her career.

---

1. **Has working at the D'Argenzio winery and tasting room gone exactly how you imagined it? If not, what were some surprises or struggles?**

"I've had the great opportunity to build D'Argenzio Winery's tasting room and wine club from scratch and it's been a wonderful experience. I have passion for what I do and do - I've created a job for myself which encompasses all the things I enjoy. Of course wine is the first, but the business aspect of the wine industry is fun, inviting, invigorating! I love working with guests, pouring them wine and creating memorable experiences, but more importantly I love making the winery successful and turning our guests into loyal wine club members that will continue to purchase wine for years to come. As a family run and operated winery, whom only sells directly through our tasting room and wine club, I'm proud to say I've build a wine club from zero members to 600 members….. of course it has not gone exactly how I've imaged it would go, but life brings it's everyday challenges which push me to continue leaning and making the best out of difficult situation. It's impossible to make everyone happy, but within bad situations, good can come out of it."

2. **What can you tell me about the Winery that sets it apart from another (nearby or of similar size)?**

"D'Argenzio Winery is a hidden gem tucked away in an urban area of Santa Rosa. Most people don't expect to walk in to a full production winery and tasting room when they first pull into our parking lot. We are an old cabinet shop, which the owner, Ray D'Argenzio grew up doing, and had a passion for winemaking which he decided to pursue as a hobby in the back of his cabinet shop. He started off with about 200 cases of zinfandel, and now we produce about 1200 cases annually, which each wine being 50-100 cases each. It's hard to find boutique family run and operated wineries now a days. There are many wineries that produce delicious wine (which I personally enjoy and advocate for), and I believe we are one of them. We only sell direct through our tasting room and to our wine club members, without any distribution.

Like other small businesses, it can be difficult to manage certain aspects of everyday protocol. I know exactly what I want our image to portray to our guests, and sometimes I find it difficult to have everyone work together as a team to make that happen. I expect every person that walks in, to feel welcome and an extension of our family. Growing up in the cabinet shop and over the last eight years as it's become a full winery and tasting room, my investment and passion has grown. If I see something done in a way I feel doesn't portray us correctly it can be stressful or upsetting, and must be managed - all part of the job! A very small example is the kind of music played in your tasting room — I think it's important to remember that it's our job to create a memorable experience for our guests. When they walk in to our small Italian winery they want to feel as if the Italian culture is encompassing them - even at a subconscious level. I've had this small issue with employees happen over and over again where they will play music that's not reflective of our winery at - I'll come in and hear reggae, pop, rock, etc.... I've recently had to make a policy to only play specific stations while our guests are visiting including Dean

Martin, Bossanova, and other similar stations. Maybe I'm a stickler, but all the small pieces of marketing to your guests while they are visiting are important - and make or break your customers."

3. **What would you tell someone who just passed their WSET Advanced (or Certified Exam with the Court) and wants to get a career at a winery?**

"Timing is everything. It's important to remember that winery/tasting rooms are a business, and managers don't want to hire unless they need help. If you're a good candidate for hire, in the right place at the right time - you will be snagged very quickly - especially for sales and hospitality. We stay in business with the selling of wine and returning customers, so I always look for someone with strong sales skills and hospitality experience. First impressions and how you shake hands has more weight than most people think it has. Any time I've compromised with these items, I've regretted it - as a hiring manager." -Breanna Tamburin, D'Argenzio Winery

---

Winemaking

Winemaking is 80% cleaning and carrying stuff, and the remaining 20% feels like College Chem. lab. Winemakers need to check PH, alcohol, total and volatile acidity, brix levels, all sometimes twice per day. Of course, winemaking is about passion, energy and harmony, but the work is more challenging that you might imagine. 3 hours of winemaking can feel sort of like 6 at the gym, depending on the time of year of course. From punch-down and pump-overs to cleaning barrels and carrying ladders, it can take a serious toll on your body. However, there are some chill days and weeks, when your day consists of just a few routine checkups to make sure your grape juice is turning into wine.

Good winemakers consider every factor, from the rocks to the sun and the wind to the rain. Along with vineyard managers, winemakers are trying to control a plant that doesn't want to be controlled. The harvest is going to come when it comes, whether you are ready for it or not. Just consider each of the four seasons over the last 5 years. Those shockingly warm winters or surprisingly cold summers create a little outfit stress for us, but can result in very serious problems throughout a vineyard. Ruined crop by rain, frost, heat or drought is all too common in winemaking.

As you may have guessed, winemaking and vineyard management has a lot to do with money. As a winery owner, you will be living off of your product and nature might get in the way of your big bonus or next family vacation. They say that good winemakers can produce a good wine in any vintage. I believe that to an extent, but the majority of the most successful wineries are those with money. That's probably why they are popular and successful, they can afford to make big changes when unexpected weather arises. Sometimes you hit a magic year when everyone's happy, the winemaker had very little struggles, and the outcome was delicious. On the flip side, wineries may fail miserably in a problematic vintage, as they simply don't have the means to recover their fruit or vines.

Well educated winemakers not only know how to properly store and maintain their product, but they know how to taste it. This is one of the many examples of how those blind tasting exams come in handy. Those who've tasted the best wines in the world are also those who know how to make the best wine in the world. They compete with their favorite producers and understand the significance of distinguishing specific varietals from specific places. For instance, if you're making Sauvignon Blanc, you wouldn't want someone telling you that it tastes like Chardonnay, right? You want it to express the best parts of the grape's features. Sauvignon Blanc should be more herbaceous than Chardonnay and lead with citrus fruit. That's why people love it and that's why they buy it.

Managing a Vineyard

So you wanna get dirty? Vineyard and viticulturist jobs are best for people who love being outdoors. You also must be able to work odd hours and have a major love of agriculture. There is a lot to learn for this type of position, but working in a vineyard is the best preparation. There are several books and schools on managing a vineyard. I suggest local schools, rather than online education, or attending courses outside of your community. The teachers likely know the area you plan to work, and can offer specific advise on dealing with weather conditions, particular soil types and more. If you choose this career, you are required to live somewhere beautiful.

Chapter 9

Other Wine Careers

Writing

Wine writing, where do I begin? Anyone can write! Start a blog, an account on the app, "Delectable," a book, whatever. However, getting paid as a wine writer takes an ample amount of education and experience, and quite possibly several connections.

Lately, however, companies have been out-sourcing blog and website content. Websites are obviously very important for wine, especially for online retailers, auctioneers, storage companies, and wine software. They often hire writers for several projects, but you might not know when they're going to reach out. They may need help writing about a particular wine or an upcoming event. It's good work when you can get it. This is unless you have a continuous writing contract, as a monthly contributor for example. If you're new to wine and a career in writing interests you, start now! Write about your process, start a blog, intern for a wine publication, apprentice for a writer, and read as much as possible.

Blogging

There are several types of wine bloggers. Some focus on the educational aspect, others mix food, travel and other alcoholic beverages. Bloggers love to write, and I only know a handful of them that actually get paid to do it. Let's think about how to make a career out of blogging. Eventually, with a big enough following, wine brands may send you free wine (sweet) to post and write about. Maybe that free bottle or case IS your payment, but like most people, I prefer my payments to come in monetary form.

If your blog has a large audience, wine brands can sell a ton of product, and will usually pay accordingly. I know a blogger that writes about wine sold through a particular online retailer. She gets paid when someone purchases one of the wines she writes about using her designated 10% discount code at checkout, "MOLLY10." Advertising is also a great way to cash out. However, you'll probably need an even larger audience in order to be approached about purchasing ad space on your blog or website.

Let's take a look at the blog, Wine Folly, for example. Madeline Puckette has been blogging in an educational and informative way for many years. She is an Advanced Sommelier with an extreme amount of experience and loads of content on regions, styles and grapes from all over the world. Now, she is capitalizing on her own educational products like posters and books.

All of her posts were originally written out of pure interest and curiosity, and we thank her greatly for sharing. However, all of this writing has resulted in tons of exposure. Her content is the leading contributor in landing her on Google's first page or even first listing. If you Google "What does Malbec taste like" don't be surprised to see her site come up first. She is probably drawing hundreds of people in daily, resulting in several paid writing jobs (not to mention help sell her own books).

If you have a blog or website, you will soon find the importance of SEO, tags, e-marketing and advertising. That's literally another book in itself, but I highly recommend it for promoting your company, services, and/or products online.

Social Media for Wine

Before diving into social media for wine, let's take a look at another industry, interior design. My husband Anthony is a stylist (mainly home furnishings and interiors) and extremely active in the social media world. Nonetheless, 90% of his new clients find him and his styling company (@zioandsons) on instagram. With over 75k followers, his clients see his previous projects and beautiful photography and want either those services, or to be featured on his account for exposure. However, styling and photographing furniture and home products is already his job. He has tons of bright and beautiful images from his weekly interior jobs. In his design-savvy, heavily visual universe, he has a lot of options and a massive audience.

Compare that to the wine industry for a minute. Wine professionals should post pictures of wine, right? Not exactly. First, the images are usually very dark, since most of us drink after the sun goes down. On top of that, pictures of wine bottles and labels aren't exactly visually pleasing. For this reason, I decided to get creative and combine the experience with videos pouring into a glass, food pairing successes, or a stylish new restaurant or wine shop. Being creative and making social media more about my life led me to gain over 10k followers in under a year. Now, that's nothing compared to my husband, but I'm getting booked through Instagram, and that's all that matters. Think less about popularity and more about profitability.

I've also found that usually, your followers want to get to know YOU. I used to post bottle pics only, afraid to get "of topic." Then, I noticed that the most successful posts are actually of me and wherever my life takes me. This doesn't work for everyone and every business, but I'm selling a service: in-home tasting classes, consulting, and content. When people reach out to me to teach a wine class, they want to see my personality and make sure it's a good fit for their event or group.

I'm also a big fan of using the right hashtags, in order to be seen by your ideal audience. If I used #wine I will likely NOT be seen by anyone searching that hashtag. This is because as my 10k account isn't big enough to get to the top/recommended posts for that tag the way that a 40k account would. Instead, I'll use hashtags with my niche, like #sommlife or #wineclass, each with under 18k posts. I try to post every day or even twice per day, as it seems to be the most successful in terms of growth. Since I am active daily, you'll likely find my images in the top 6 of the hashtags I use. Therefore, anyone searching those tags will probably see my posts and hopefully interact in a positive way.

Speaking of interaction, know the importance of engagement. It's called social media, be social. Answer questions, tell someone you like their feed, whatever. Go through similar accounts to yours, find people and companies you would like to work with, then like, follow, and comment. Be friends, and then offer your new friends little gifts like free wine, fun blog posts, this book, etc. Campaigns have really worked wonders in gaining a substantial following and of course, new business.

In the wine industry, you see a lot of tweeting, and a little less facebooking. I have been told that tweeting is very important if you want your business to be seen. I tweet sometimes and just for this reason, but I genuinely like Instagram much more. Having a Facebook page for your business is very important, as you can invite friends to like it, rate your company, charge clients, and even pay to promote your posts. It is quite beneficial if you own or are starting a wine-related business.

Wine Apps

Wine Apps can be fun, informative, and a fantastic way to keep track of what you like or taste. Vivino for example, is often used by my peers for price comparisons, ratings and reviews. It's a great way to learn and rate wines for your personal enjoyment. Another great app, with similar scan-and-rate technology is Delectable. I prefer this app due to their easy journaling function. It is especially helpful for studious newbies as they attend tastings and classes. These Apps are here to help consumers, rather than act as a way of promoting yourself. However, I forsee this changing in the future, especially as new companies search for employees. Your wine profile on these Apps might act as a tool for reputable companies to find you. In fact, an App-active friend of mine has proven herself a respectable industry professional by sharing her wine journal and tasting notes. Viewing one's tasting notes is an excellent way to pinpoint their experience, personality, and approach to wine, in my opinion.

Sensory Analysts and Professional Wine Tasters

Want to literally get paid to taste wine? Great, but without decades of experience, you better be a Master Sommelier or Master of Wine. Not many people in the world get paid to do this, and they probably work for Wine Advocate, Wine Enthusiast or another review company. This career also involves an immense amount of writing, which is why you're tasting in the first place. The goal is to inform readers, sellers, and buyers and hopefully increase sales for the wineries rated highly.

I'm often asked about the process of tasting wine. How does one do it, or become good at it? First, it doesn't just either happen for you or not. Unless you're in the 1% who *cannot* taste, successful tasting involves years of practice evaluating wine. When I was 21, the only tasting notes I could grasp were lemons for white and cherries for red. Then, a seasoned Wine Director told me, "Sure, every white has lemons and every red has cherries, but what else?" Frustrated and impatient, I assumed I was doomed forever because I really couldn't taste anything for quite some time.

Then, at one of my first restaurant jobs, the servers and sommeliers were asked to bring in specific ingredients for a wine training. Everyone had been assigned a different fruit, flower, spice or vegetable. I got mushrooms. There I was at the bar with my white mushrooms, looking at all of these ingredients across the bar. There were raspberries, roses, thyme, blackberries, tomatoes, daffodils, basil and much more, as there were nearly twenty of us. Then, the Head Sommelier put 3 wines in front of everyone and said, "Each of these wines have particular markers that each of you brought today. Now, figure out which descriptor goes with which wine." The exercise was "blind," meaning that we had no idea what the wines were. A few of us studying servers kind of knew what to look for, as we had learned the markers and flavors that most people would associate with certain grapes.

After 15 minutes or so, we all wrote down what we thought the wines were, after smelling and tasting the ingredients we brought. We ended up opening several other wines that could be associated to these ingredients, and this was one of the best tastings I'd ever been to. You tend to forget what to think about when you're tasting wine. Instead, think about every common descriptor you can. Consider fruit, flowers, spices, herbs, vegetables, and literally list these options in your mind until something jumps out at you. Then, put the most powerful ones together and consider what grapes usually have these markers. Perhaps you put them in little "families." For instance, I group Sauvignon Blanc, Grüner Veltliner and Albariño together because they have very similar tasting notes. With time, you can taste them apart by focusing on the tertiary aromas. Grüner Veltliner sets itself apart from the "family" with tertiary aromas of asparagus and green peas. These notes are quite difficult for a novice to identify, but taste enough Gruner and you'll always pick up on the veggies.

Brand Ambassadors

This is another awesome career option and usually does not require massive amounts of experience, though it *can*. Growing wineries will hire an Ambassador for a number of reasons, but usually in order to build and sustain relationships with key accounts. These wineries must be willing and able to sell a lot of wine and usually own their own vineyards and have serious financial backing.

Beverage Brand Ambassadors usually organize the necessary samples for tastings and sponsored events. For this reason, some brands require PR experience and especially like to hire employees that come with a book of clients. Big brands and groups of brands are constantly planning and executing large-scale events, some complete with industry influencers or even celebrities.

This position may also require analyzing sales data, distribution activity, sales stats and even the installation of marketing materials. Like any industry, this can all depend on the size and organization of the company, but this career is best for presenters and those who enjoy training others. Brand Ambassadors are required to convey the brand message each and every day, as well as train the sales staff and consumers on each product.

One potential downfall is that you'll rarely taste or talk about anything other than that brand. You should always know plenty about wine for presentation purposes. Your audience will likely compare the varietal choices and winemaking decisions to other brands and/or regions of the world. If this sounds like you, an Advanced Certificate with WSET or a CSW Certificate would probably suffice.

Chapter 10

Wine Education and How to Teach a Class!

If you decide to go the Educator route, there's one lesson you need to learn right now. Teaching is extremely repetitive and it's usually surrounded by the basics, whether you like it or not. Let's face it, if they knew about wine, they wouldn't be paying you to teach them about it. Sure, Master Somms teach advanced courses all the time, but I don't know any who have made a career out of just that. The truth is, there hasn't been enough of a need for advanced education as a full time career – yet!

Having taught over 300 wine classes, here's a bit of advice: First and foremost, you must be able to answer ANY question, especially the geographical ones. It doesn't hurt knowing your producers either. There's bound to be some finance bro whose lawyer daddy taught him all about Napa Cabernet. This dude will most likely ask the question, "Have you ever had Screaming Eagle?" This is where I say "Yep, so good." Question? Not really, just either testing your knowledge, showing off, or both. Try waiting to roll your eyes until after the tasting.

Then, there's the obvious groups you'll find who couldn't care less about wine, they just really need a new or creative excuse to get hammered. The group of sorority girls who see each other once a month, the Tinder couple making out in the back. If you're pouring, they will come. I've seen it all, including a young woman who took a bite out of her wine glass. I think she got the wine confused with the cheese.

My favorite audience is the older couple who clearly wants to learn about wine. After 35 years of marriage, they're pretty over each other and would rather work on building their relationship with wine. They're attentive, interested, and don't care how embarrassing the wine question they decide to ask is, or who the hell hears it. They're getting their money's worth and not once will you find them fondling each other under the table.

Once, I taught a private wine class in the cellar for a couple that ended in a proposal. I had done about ten of these, but none of them ended like this. Normally, candles and flowers fill the room and the young woman smiles upon entering, knowing that this was *it*. The groom-to-be always planned the proposal using "engagement ideas" websites. So, I always knew and my acting skills needed to be on point. "Awe, you are such a sweet boyfriend to book a private tasting! Aren't you guys sooooo Cuuuute!" After about an hour of going through 6 wines, I'd always leave the room to "get another bottle." In reality, I'd stand behind the door, creepily listening to the proposal. She cries, I smile, give them 10 minutes to make out, then come back and congratulate with Champagne.

This time, however, things didn't go as planned. She freaking said No! I couldn't believe my ears. What?? I heard her say "David, you know I've only ever thought of you as a friend, how could you do this? Are you trying to make me feel bad?" It was so totally odd. I knew that I had to come in and pretend I didn't hear anything, so I turned on my inner actress and pretended like I wasn't creeping out in the cellar. "Alright, here's that bottle. Have you ever tried Cab franc?" "No, please tell us about it!" What the hell, Okay... I went on talking about wine for another 40 minutes, just wondering about this "couple" and how she could have led him on long enough to buy a ring. Point of the story is this: presenting is a performance and no matter the weird situation, the show must go on. Have back up plans and feel comfortable going wherever your audience takes you. If she wants to talk about the Loire Valley for 40 minutes because she just turned down a marriage proposal, just go with it.

TEACHING FORMAT EXAMPLE: My go-to for basic 101 classes, but this could be done 10 million different ways. I highly recommend you find your style and emphasize on your favorite points.

1. **Intro**

    - Welcome the group, give them your name and about 30 seconds on yourself while making the group feel comfortable. Example: "Hi and thanks for having me, my name is Hillary, I'm a Certified Sommelier. I've worked in wine for 10 years, but I don't know everything! It's a big world of wine out there with 3,000 different grape varietals that you would never need to know. I'm here to give you the basics so that you can order properly, get exactly what you want at the wine store. So, *please* feel free to ask LOTS of questions, and I'll do my best to answer them for you."

    - Then, mention the tasting format. Example: "We will be tasting left to right, white to red, with a short intermission where I'll pour some more wine for you."

    - Always ask, "Who's taken a wine class before?" Find out if anyone in the room knows anything about wine. Usually you will get a few who've been to wineries, maybe even a class or two. If there is a seasoned wine lover in the room, figure out when you can focus on them a bit. Perhaps while the others are talking, you can get a little geeky with them. For another way to figure out if there are any less-than-novices in the room, ask "Who knows what the 3 grapes are in Champagne??" This is great because you will likely start with a sparkling wine in the tasting or upon arrival.

- Then, mention the difference between sparkling, white, and red. The process, maceration, options for making a wine bubbly, pink, etc. (This Intro should take no longer than 15 minutes, people are here
- to taste!)

2. **The Tasting**

- Go through the 4 S's of tasting wine: sight, smell, sip, and savor.
- Explain acidity, tannin, body, balance, and finish.
- Smell and taste each wine and discuss the characteristics, structure, and ask the group their opinion about each. For example, "What kinds of fruits, flowers, herbs or *anything* else comes to mind upon your initial sniff or taste?" If the group is being quiet, mention your personal tasting notes and/or common markers of the grape or place that you aren't picking up on. Modesty is key because wine really freaks people out for some reason. Mentioning these descriptors helps the group speak up, "Oh yea, I totally get pineapple here."

- Test them a little bit. I've found that the general public is quite fascinated by blind tasting, why not make them guess. This is usually best at the end of the class, after you have taught them how to distinguish wines. For example, "If you think the wine tastes like blackberries, which varietals did I mention that usually smell and taste like that?"

3. **The Conclusion**

- Answer questions, and be ready for these FAQs: How do I store my wine properly? How do I read an Italian/French/German label? How can I become a Sommelier? Have you been to Bordeaux/Tuscany/Champagne? Have you seen Bottle Shock/Somm 1/ Somm 2/ Sideways?

Chapter 11

More Advice for Working in the Wine Industry

Mentioned already, company culture is extremely important, in any industry. I've seen the good, the bad and the ugly. Here are two examples of restaurants (names are not real, stories are) and exactly what they did (and are currently doing) right and very wrong.

Restaurant 1: Pop Off, a small wine bar in the West Village with a decent menu, mainly comprised of small bites. Opened 2 years ago, this expensive joint is in a great location and stays busy most of the time.

Restaurant 2: Parkside, another relatively high end wine bar in Union Square Park. Also a great location, this 2 and a half year old restaurant has a slightly larger wine list and dinner menu, also busy most of the time.

As you can see, both businesses are relatively new, busy and in great locations. The difference is that Pop Off has a very quick turn-over of employees and Parkside still has the same team of Somms and servers since opening. Pop Off has had to spend precious time and money on job posting, interviewing, training, and several other managerial issues. Parkside has never had to post a job advertisement and relies solely on referrals in attaining top quality employees.

So, what is Parkside doing right and Pop Off doing wrong? Two Words: Company Culture. Parkside is an all-around comfortable work setting and anyone can pick up on the happiness of the staff. The management treat employees with respect, as well as offer an appropriate wage and vacation days. Pop Off has drama. The managers are constantly reprimanding employees in public. Everyone can feel the tension in this hostile environment. Management doesn't greet you with a smile upon walking in, they make you feel *their* stress.

We all know the importance of treating others as you would like to be treated, so how does this keep happening, especially in the service industry? I think it's up to us to end it. If you're having issues, don't bring them to work. Keep to yourself if you need to, get the job done, and go home and cry, talk shit, whatever. I asked all 8 employees of Pop Off why they left the wine bar, each one pointed at the owner and/or management. Three of them had the exact same response actually, "You'd walk into work every day, never knowing what kind of mood (the boss) was in." Not a fun kind of guessing game. So, if you feel you may be working in a Pop Off environment, get the hell out. Life's too short for that and most people aren't crazy, but a lot of restaurant owners are.

Networking is vitally important. This happens at events, tastings, groups (Guild Somm), Industry Night, etc. Keep an email list! It's so important to build a few client lists. 1.) People who buy wine, who may eventually buy from you. 2.) Retailers/Restaurants you know, who may be a good contact for selling, working with, etc.

1. Get a mentor! Ask every question you have, taste with them, taste in front of them, ask them questions, set up monthly meetings. Guild Somm is meant to be a community and people really do want to help! My mentor does exactly what I do, but she's in California and I'm in New York, so we aren't in any kind of competition.

2. Dude, be nice… Rude Somms are always made fun of behind their backs by cool Somms. I can't tell you how many people in this industry have rolled their eyes or turned up their nose at me, especially when I started out.

   I once worked with this bartender/mixologist asshole. He used to call me "Hillary Hairbrain, all hair and no brain." Turned out he was just jealous that I had hair (yes, he was very bald), but his rude, ridiculous comments only made him disliked by the other industry professionals. Finally, his attitude got him kicked out of the bar during his shift. It's just lame and completely uncalled for. Remember, it's a small industry (for now), and even working in Manhattan, you would be shocked with how quickly word gets around. Nobody knows everything. If someone knew all 3,000 grape varietals indigenous to Italy, I'd feel very sorry for them.

On top of that, the Court of Master Sommeliers take snobbiness very seriously and has definitely failed candidates for it. Humility will get you points these days, when a bad yelp review could cost you your job. The whole being nice thing has really taken off lately, and I thank the internet. Don't be a dick, just don't.

3. Your colleagues are usually pretty cool. The people I've worked with lately have been ridiculously laid back and never in competition with me. They see what I'm doing, I see what they're doing and we help and wish well for each other. I think that many people in wine understand that there are plenty of restaurants, stores, and distribution companies in their city and with a little training, they can easily find plenty of great career options.

4. Don't get high on your own supply. Many of my peers in this industry have fallen into having questionable drinking problems. At the end of the day, drinking on the job is not cool. I know several professionals who have lost their reputation, their job, or had to

seek professional help. When you're tasting wine professionally, it's tempting to swallow. Maybe you're having a rough day, bored, whatever it is, you'll likely start a reputation as a lush. Again, it's a small industry! So please, spit, especially at tastings. When reps see you swallow, they might not take you seriously. Maybe you won't get to try that back vintage reserve in their bag because you look like a wasted newbie.

Let me tell you about a Captain at one of the restaurants I worked in very early on in my career. Jenny (let's call her) liked to work pretty tipsy. She made sure to "taste" every glass of wine she was going to pour, no matter if the Sommelier deemed it "good to pour" Even on my first day, she offered that we take "wine shots" while the owner went to the kitchen.

Jenny was a drunk, but she was "studying." Every chance to taste (or chug) was a learning experience in her eyes. Months later, after failing her Certified Sommelier Exam, I heard several staff members call her "The Whale Shark." From one server to the next, "well maybe if she wasn't Whale-Sharking everyday she could have passed." Now, if you've ever seen a Whale Shark (or swam with them – which is an amazing and highly recommended experience), you'll notice their massive mouths, opening as wide as possible, in order to catch plankton. That's just what Jenny did every shift, to make sure no one noticed how quick that glass of wine went down her throat. Not only was Jenny eventually fired, she maintained her reputation as The Whale Shark. At age 40, I've heard she still hasn't passed her wine exams and has been fired from the last few restaurants she's worked.

5. The Unfortunate Reality of Male Domination. Truth is, this is a male-dominated industry by far (for now). That can come with a testosterone-driven work dynamic. Young women that are new to the industry usually get a rude awakening of insensitivity or even public hostility.

    At one job, the manager and owner (both males) would call each other disgusting names, literally screaming in earshot of not only the female staff, but in front of customers. I never understood why the hell some men (and women) can't understand the repercussions of actions like this.

    I used to work with a lovely event coordinator who truly adored her job and the company where we worked together. One day, the owner went berserk on her about something quite ridiculous: candle placement. He yelled "can you tell me what's wrong with this picture??" Apparently there weren't enough candles. Each week after that one instance, she would bring up his incompetence to lead the company and how she wants to find a new job. She ended up leaving the company one month later, after job-searching every day after that one incident. My only advice is to get out before it gets ugly, and try your hardest to feel the vibe and get pick up on cues during the interview. The signs are there. Talk to some women in the company, do they seem happy? If not, is their attitude due to the men (or women) at the company or is it an outside factor? I think we all know that there are gentlemen and there are shitheads. Either find the gentlemen or only work for women.

6. On working remotely: For me, it's been the absolute best thing ever. I've found that I work ridiculously more efficiently from home. Eliminating my 40 minute each-way commute, and the daily hassle of finding something to wear has freed up time and money. Goodbye unlimited metro card, $14 salads, and "work clothes." Now, the option of an 11 o'clock jog completely jumpstarts my productivity and inspiration. Offices are also much more distracting for me, from chatty coworkers and unnecessary meetings to the horrible music and constant room temperature frustration. Now, this obviously doesn't work for everyone. Many feel very distracted at home, with pets, kids, television, etc.

I forsee the option to work remotely becoming more popular in the wine industry. Not only are companies saving on office furniture, but the internet has allowed us to see exactly how hard everyone is working. My friend, Hannah works for a large Hotel group that does not allow any of their employees to work remotely. Hannah told me that she spends around 6 hours per day on social media and shopping websites. She has to be there, but she doesn't have to work more than 2 hours per day? Tell me how that makes sense. So, what kinds of wine jobs have options to work remote? Sales, buying, writing, research, everything. However, very few companies offer it right now but I predict that will change.

Chapter 12

CHEERS, You're Done!

You're done! If you haven't poured yourself a glass yet, do that now, I'll wait. I covered all kinds of wine careers, not everything, but I hope you're closer to your goals and where you plan to go, stay, or explore. I have to say, 10 years later, I undeniably love working in wine. I may not be rich in monetary terms, but I absolutely adore what I do. I get to travel, learn, write and help people understand wine. I've learned how to consult newcomers and businesses due to the variety of jobs I've had.

I was approached recently about writing this and asked if I was giving myself competition by educating the next wave of professionals in wine. That's just insane to me, really? Are we all exactly the same and want all the same positions? Hell no, the world doesn't work like that. Don't ever feel threatened by others' successes, there's plenty of glasses in this bottle, not just four and a half. This industry is not a secret. Wine has been around since 300 BC! There are so many different options in the wine industry, after a little education and experience.

So what does the future look like for wine professionals? Whatever we make it. I predict, with full access to all information on the internet, the wine industry is going to become more approachable. With more of us travelling every year, we attain a better understanding of different cultures. I forsee wine becoming more of a way of life for Americans, similar to how it's always been in Europe. Also, with so many up-and-coming regions, I think that we'll be able to spend less to get great wine. This also stands for craft beer, spirits and sake.

So far, I've found the wine industry extremely rewarding. My mind has been blown time and time again when I consider the history, geology, geography and the wonderful experience of being able to taste beautiful wines from around the world. Maybe it's the region that makes some wine so wonderful or maybe it's the team behind the production. Either way, I don't see myself wanting to stop learning any time soon. I have found my calling and I want to help interested women and men find their place here, or at least figure out if it's for them.

Please know that this guide is not the be-all end-all and every day I'm hearing about a new wine career. My buddies in the tech industry have especially been showing me that! So start somewhere, get out there, be different, and discover as much as possible.

Cheers!

Made in the USA
Middletown, DE
01 November 2018